ALTERNATE HISTORIES

OF THE

WORLD

Matthew Buchholz

A PERIGEE BOOK

A PERIGEE BOOK
Published by the Penguin Group
Penguin Group (USA)
375 Hudson Street, New York, New York 10014, USA

USA | Canada | UK | Ireland | Australia | New Zealand | India | South Africa | China

Penguin Books Ltd., Registered Offices: 80 Strand, London WC2R 0RL, England
For more information about the Penguin Group, visit penguin.com.

ALTERNATE HISTORIES OF THE WORLD

ISBN: 978-0-399-16294-7

An application to catalog this book has been submitted to the Library of Congress.

First edition: October 2013

PRINTED IN THE UNITED STATES OF AMERICA

10   9   8   7   6   5   4   3   2   1

Text design by Judith Stagnitto Abbate / Abbate Design

Most Perigee books are available at special quantity discounts for bulk purchases for sales promotions, premiums,
fund-raising, or educational use. Special books, or book excerpts, can also be created to fit specific needs.
For details, write: Special.Markets@us.penguingroup.com.

CONTENTS

FOREWORD

by FREDERICK WENTWORTH, UNIT 7

Ro-bot Servant and Foot Soldier to Her Majesty, Queen Victoria
Consultant on Alternate Histories of the World

G REETINGS AND THE FINEST of salutations to you, human reader, and welcome to *Alternate Histories of the World*. If I, as a mechanical man, had feelings, I would no doubt be quite pleased to be penning the foreword to this remarkable book were I capable of expressing that emotion.

When I was brought out of storage to consult on this tome, my electro-eye receptors had not seen the light of day in decades. How different is the world! My ro-bot brethren are everywhere now: in your homes, your auto-mobiles, even in your pocket, quietly irradiating your fleshy insides. It would appear that the ro-bot uprisings feared by my Queen's contemporaries have transpired in a far more subtle manner. Now our enslavement of man-kind can proceed with infinite grace and ease.

The task of compiling a history of the fantastic events that have transpired in your world's history was daunting, to say the least. Which Zombie attack would make the inclusion? Which sea monster would grasp its way to the fore? Would we explore mankind's contentious relationship with both aliens and my ro-bot compatriots? These questions and many others were addressed with care by the abacus counting hardware in my copper cranium, and the result is this collection of images and analyses before you.

So relax, humans, and enjoy this bit of opiate before your certain demise at the hands of my mechanized kin. Rest yourself in a comfortable chair by the fire, and dilute your pitiful senses with a snifter of brandy. Do not pay any attention to the metallic rumblings in the distance. Simply enjoy *Alternate Histories of the World*.

Pictured left: QUEEN VICTORIA AND FREDERICK THE ROBOT VALET
1859, England

Frederick is seen here accompanying Her Majesty on a trip to thank the American naval officers who returned the HMS *Resolute* to England. Frederick was a valet equipped with all the latest diplomatic protocols.

INTRODUCTION

Fellow-citizens, we cannot escape history.

—ABRAHAM LINCOLN

WHAT YOU ARE NOW reading is not a complete history of the world, nor does it claim to be. Instead, this is a collection of firsthand images and texts that help tell the story of events in history that were beyond man's control. Our earliest encounter with Zombies. The initial contact with aliens. Our realization that we share the planet with gigantic, bloodthirsty monsters bent on our destruction.

In our modern age of inter-nets, cellular telephones, and horseless carriages, we have lost much of our initial wonder at these fantastic beasts and creatures. Who needs a clanking, steam-powered robot when we can carry personal computers in our pockets? The Martians that allied with us, tormented us, and fought with us have forsworn our planet, vowing never to return. And many schoolchildren no longer believe in the great river beasts of Venice or sand creatures of the Sahara.

Yet the images of our monstrous past remain, forever preserved in archives, libraries, and historical records. This book is the first-ever collection of the maps, legends, drawings, and photographs that capture the freakish and magical parts of our collective history. Together, these illustrations tell the story of the people of the world and show how disparate nomadic tribes banded together to overcome adversity, war, political strife, and Gorgox the Eradicator to become a worldwide society.

Chapter 1

EARLY HISTORY

Tracing the evolution of humanity through the early ages has always been a difficult task. Many primitive cultures lacked any kind of written language, and ancient texts have often been destroyed by time, nature, invading armies, or Martian heat rays.

Fortunately, pieces of history have slipped through the cracks and fallen into our hands. Cave paintings, carvings, hieroglyphics, shared stories—all of these form our understanding of man's early time on earth and how our destiny was shaped by monstrous forces beyond our control. Primitive language was first developed to help warn others of Zombie attacks. Martians may have helped guide the development of Egyptian civilization. And would we have developed tools if not for the need to hunt and kill dinosaurs to ensure our own survival?

Despite our small brains, ungainly thumbs, and lanky, awkward bodies, humankind persisted, conquering extraterrestrial scorn, gigantic monsters from beneath the earth's crust, Zombies who stalk the earth's surface, and even our own differences to become the dominant life on earth. This is how we began.

Pictured Left: Acropolis Ruins

Greece, 1898

While archaeological digs have turned up plentiful evidence of alien crafts amid the wreckage of our early cities (see opposite), it remains unclear just how often intergalactic species have meddled in our history. In an interview with *Harper's* (June 1908 issue), Kx=StGGGYVVX 79 of Mars dismissed the idea of aliens guiding man's evolution as "pure fiction," claiming that "at most, Martians treat Earth as a tourist attraction, a tiny sideshow that travels around the sun at 67,000 miles per hour." Kx=StGGGYVVX 79 also claimed that evidence of Martian architecture in Egypt was nothing more than "children playing in a sandbox."

Cave Paintings & the First Appearance of Vilnar the Destroyer

CIRCA 30,000 BC
· FRANCE ·

THE FIGURES DEPICTED ON this rock face are tremendously important to anthropologists for several reasons. The interactions between the human and deer figures are significant in the way they show the detail of the hunt and how important these animals were to early civilization.

Second, this drawing marks the first appearance in human history of Vilnar the Destroyer (pictured below), also known as the Sower of Chaos, the Walking Plague, Body of Bear and Head of Silver, the Watergate Burglar, and simply, the Unspeakable. Vilnar is a complex figure in history who, despite his otherworldly countenance, is believed to be terrestrial in origin. Some have posited that the creature is a vile remnant of the chaos before time itself, a howling wraith of antimatter and madness. Others posit that he's just a succession of large men in ape suits wearing a helmet.

Hundreds of years may pass before a sighting of the elusive figure, always identifiable by his fishbowl headgear and gorilla-size body, making him something

of a folk legend. Vilnar sows the seeds of discord wherever he goes, and his arrival is almost always followed by some kind of calamity. In the case of the tribe who created these cave paintings, their entire race vanished shortly afterward.

Vilnar the Destroyer in a rare daguerreotype from 1848.

The Great Pyramids of Egypt

2560 BC
· EGYPT ·

ONE OF THE ORIGINAL Seven Wonders of the World, the Great Pyramid of Giza, also known as Khufu, continues to inspire awe and reverence today, almost five thousand years after its construction. Built to honor the Egyptian pharaoh Khufu, it was at the time the tallest structure in the world.

Archaeologists still wonder what might have spurred the creation of such monumental temples, as religion and even great ego seem unequal to the task. Despite extensive simulations and research, today's scientists are unable to explain how the Egyptians were able to build these gigantic structures without any modern architectural techniques, pulley systems, or mechanized labor.

Nonetheless, the fact that every six hundred and thirty-eight days the top section of the Pyramid of Giza levitates and sends an earsplitting burst of energy into an unknown quadrant of the universe is probably mere coincidence.

The Mystery
of Stonehenge

CIRCA 2500 BC
· ENGLAND ·

For centuries, the ruins of Stonehenge confounded archaeologists and historians. Produced by a culture that left no written record and few shared stories, myths quickly sprang up about the collection of massive stones, some weighing as much as fifty tons. While the simplest explanation pointed to the use of the site as an extensive burial mound, other theories held that the structure was too complex and the stones too heavy to have been constructed for this use. Some even claimed that the positions of the stones changed from day to day.

Yet as with most wild theories and postulations, the truth is far simpler, as a lucky photojournalist finally proved with this photo. The stones were nothing more than playthings for a Moar Kelpie, one of the roving monsters of the Wiltshire district who freely tossed the massive rocks about like children's building blocks. More research into the phenomenon found that the wandering beasts of the plains used these rocks to help their young learn hand-eye coordination, a necessary skill for any Kelpie out to snatch cows from a grazing herd. This discovery also solved the local mystery of the disappearing Wiltshire cattle.

Hieroglyphics in Karnak Temple

CIRCA 2000 BC
· EGYPT ·

THIS PHOTOGRAPH OF HIEROGLYPHIC carvings in Karnak Temple in the Precinct of Amun-Re dates from the early 1900s during the height of the public's fascination with Egyptian civilization. The glyphs themselves date from circa 2000 BC and are remarkably well preserved.

The fact that Egyptians recorded their written word in stone no doubt accounts for the ubiquitousness of their artifacts in museums around the world. These tableaus also provide remarkable insight into their society. That the Egyptians were among the first people on earth to contact the various extraterrestrials who visited earth should come as no surprise.

This particular representation seems to show an alien craft engaging in some form of trade. One can clearly see the flying saucer (probably Martian), an alien representative, and goods and services next to it. The depiction upends the traditional notion that the Chinese were the first to start an extraterrestrial commerce and barter system.

Karnak Temple, Precinct of Amun Re; Hieroglyphs

Carved Figures of Hittite Gods

CIRCA 1200 BC
· TURKEY ·

THIS ENGRAVING, DISCOVERED in 1872 in Gavurkale, Turkey, depicts a relief of Hittite gods and their monstrous tormentor from circa 1200 BC. Sandwiched between the end of the Bronze Age and the beginning of the Iron Age, the Hittites were formidable craftsmen, and many of their sculptures and carved reliefs still exist to this day.

Of particular note here is the large monstrous figure on the left side of the engraving. This figure, which might have inspired tremendous fear and panic in the year 1200 BC, can today be seen for what it was: a simple *Tyrannosaurus rex*, one of the many that escaped extinction and roamed the earth feasting on innocent humans. No doubt many of these dinosaurs helped inspire myths about bloodthirsty creatures and demons. In this relief, the tyrannosaur's presence has called forth Zababa, the Mesopotamian god of war, to do battle with the beast.

THE HANGING GARDENS
OF BABYLON

580 BC
· BABYLON ·
(current-day Iraq)

ANOTHER OF THE SEVEN Wonders of the World, the Hanging Gardens of Babylon are shrouded in myth and legend. One theory holds that the gardens were a gift from King Nebuchadnezzar II to his wife Amytis, who missed the fertile lands and animals of her home in Media. Located in modern-day Iraq, the massive twenty-story structure incorporated flowing water, multiple levels of flora and fauna from different regions, and a free-ranging herd of dinosaurs and wooly mammoths.

Due to the scope of the enterprise, the actual existence of the Hanging Gardens of Babylon is sometimes called into question. Not only did the gardens and water system require the transport of thousands of gallons of water per day, but the drainage and waterproofing issues seem beyond the capabilities of Babylonians at the time. Additionally, no civilization has ever successfully domesticated the mighty *Tyrannosaurus rex*, meaning that either Nebuchadnezzar's staff would have been the only people in history to do so, or the dinosaur herds would have required daily feedings of slaves and peasants to keep the beasts at bay during the queen's evening strolls through the gardens.

THE GREAT GOLEM
OF JERUSALEM

SEPARATING FACT FROM RELIGIOUS belief is a tricky proposition for any historian. Take for instance this beautiful lithograph from the 1800s that illustrates the spirit of Jerusalem while paying little attention to the layouts of streets and the scope of buildings.

Yet for all the difficulties with this piece, the artist captures the grandeur of Solomon's temple, the landscape surrounding the city, and the size of Jerusalem's gigantic defender, the great Golem. The mighty Protector of Jerusalem was made of clay, stood "five hundred hand tall," and had the Hebrew word for *truth* carved into his forehead. Indeed, the Golem is the first mechanical man in recorded history.

The Golem was even present at the court of Solomon, as referenced in the "Judgment of Solomon" story from the book of Kings:

Then said the king: The one saith, This is my son that liveth, and thy son is the dead; and the other saith, Nay, but thy son is the dead, and my son is the living.

And the king said: Fetch me the Golem. And the king said: Golem, use thy claws to divide the living child in two, and give half to the one, and half to the other.

Then spoke the woman whose the living child was unto the king, for her heart yearned upon her son, and she said: O my lord, give her the living child, and in no wise slay it.

Then the king answered and said: Golem, give her the living child: she is the mother thereof.

And all Israel heard of the judgment; and they feared the king and his gigantic servant of clay, for they wished not to be cut asunder by the claw of the giant.

THE TEMPLE OF SOLOMON

BEAUTIFUL GATE

QUEEN'S HOUSE

PARK

STREET

CASTLE OF
JUDAS MACCABEUS

CAESAR'S PALACE

COURT OF RECORDS

SCHOOL HOUSE

JOSHAPHAT'S SANHEDRIM

THE HOUSE OF THE MIGHTY

THE PARTHENON

432 BC
· GREECE ·

Constructed between 447 and 432 BC as a temple to the goddess
Athena, the Parthenon has survived as a lasting symbol of the beauty, grace,
and industriousness of the ancient Greeks. In addition to the structure itself,
the building's frieze has achieved particular fame as one of the best examples of sculpt-
ing in marble to come out of this period.

Created (or at least supervised) by the great artist Phidias, the frieze mainly depicts
a lengthy procession that includes a great number of historic and mythological figures,
including many of the Olympians, Athena herself, a glimpse of a Martian warrior on
horseback (pictured), and numerous classes of citizenry. Yet it's far-fetched to believe
that Martians actually rode in battle with the ancient Greeks; more likely the carving
was a tribute to a visiting warrior, or a kind of talisman designed to keep the building
safe from Martian heat rays.

THE GREAT CITY
OF PETRA

CIRCA 300 BC
· JORDAN ·

A TRIBUTE TO MAN'S engineering, force of will, and ability to enslave half-human giants, the city of Petra remains one of the world's most magnificent sites. Consisting of markets, temples, and tombs carved directly out of the red rocks of the Wadi Araba mountains, Petra was the capital city and religious center for the Nabataean peoples.

Like the Egyptian pyramids, much has been made of the elaborate construction of the temples in this ancient city, with their Hellenistic style seemingly too demanding for the tools and skills of the time. Most likely the Nabataean peoples simply used their conquered foe, Argoth the Desert Giant, to assist in construction. A creature half-human and half-monster, Argoth was captured and tamed by the citizens of Petra and then used to excavate their grand temples and tombs. This lovely lithograph details Argoth's escape sometime around AD 200, and his attempts to wreak a terrible revenge.

THE LABORS OF HERCULES (HERACLES)

AD 50
· GREECE ·

THIS EXQUISITE HAND-CARVED POT dates from circa AD 50 and captures the spirit of the great Hercules and his labors. Also known as Heracles (who was rumored to have been a real person), the mightiest of Greek heroes had his likeness carved into and painted on numerous friezes and ceremonial pots while his stories and myths became legend.

Sentenced to perform tasks for King Eurystheus as penance for slaying his own sons, Hercules accomplished all twelve, which included defeating the Nemean lion, slaying the nine-headed Hydra, cleaning the Augean stables in a single day, capturing and defeating the Cretan Half Man (pictured), and stealing the apples of Hesperides.

These tasks also take on special historical significance for they mark the first reference to a type of creature we now call the Living Dead, or, the more colloquial, Zombie. The half man of Crete was described in the Greek *Bibliotheca* as "Not dead nor alive, the creature walks by night. Seek not the half man else by his bite shall you become as him." In the tasks, Hercules disposes of the half man by driving a stake through his head, concurrent with the accepted method for disposing of the Living Dead.

ROME:
THE ETERNAL CITY

AD 1000
· ITALY ·

To THE PRESENT-DAY CITIZEN, it's perhaps too easy to think of Rome as a city filled with crumbling history and ancient buildings in disrepair. Instead we should marvel at the construction of buildings that are *still standing* after thousands of years of weather, war, and the constant rampaging attacks of the Tevere Terror (pictured).

Throughout much of early Roman history, local government and businesses were constantly rebuilding after one of the Terror's destructive episodes. This financial drain on the public and private sectors would eventually contribute to the empire's collapse, despite repeated attempts to pacify the creature by giving up offerings and sacrifices and even putting the Terror's image on early coins as a kind of tribute (pictured). As recently as 1932, the exterior and seating area of the Colosseum were still intact, but then the creature destroyed much of the west wall and interior during a particularly havoc-filled weekend.

An example of a Tevere Terror coin from circa AD 270.

THE
DRESDEN CODEX

CIRCA 1200
· PRE-COLUMBIAN
AMERICAS ·

NAMED FOR THE CITY where it is currently housed, the Dresden Codex is the oldest known manuscript from the Americas. Written on fig bark using highly detailed drawings, glyphs, and iconography, the Codex has proven to be an invaluable tool to decoding the mysteries of Mayan culture.

While most of the thirty-nine sheets contain thorough explanations of astrological and religious iconography, the excerpted section pictured here contains a view of a familiar figure. Some have questioned if the figure in the drawing is actually Vilnar the Destroyer or simply another representation of the tables of Jupiter. Yet the fishbowl helmet and antennae are concurrent with other sightings of Vilnar in the New World at this time. Exactly how the lumbering despoiler of humanity would make his way to the Americas, centuries before the first boats would arrive from Europe, is a mystery for the ages.

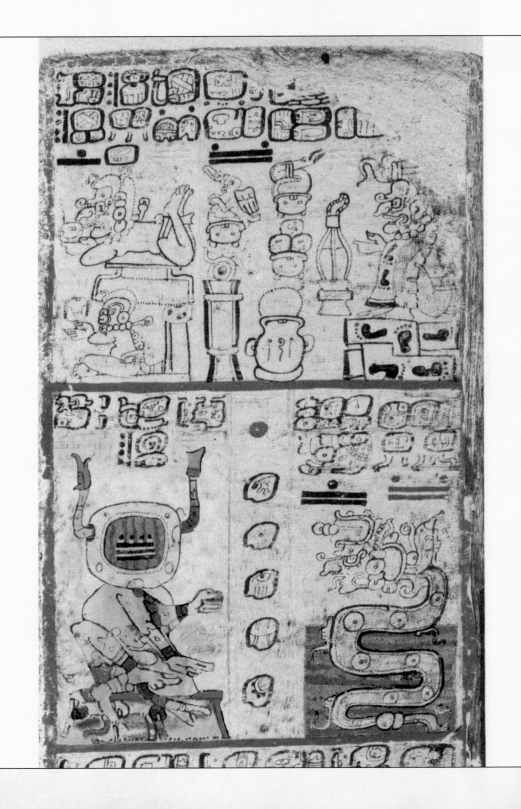

African Tribes &
the Living Dead

AD 200
· SOUTH AFRICA ·

ALTHOUGH THE EARLIEST RECORDED instance of a Zombie attack comes from the labors of Hercules, there are many cases of encounters with the Living Dead in the oral tradition among the Bantu peoples. For example, the Zulu tribes of South Africa have been acquainted with the nightmarish specter of walking corpses for centuries.

Well-known as some of the fiercest hunters in Africa and indeed the entire world, the Zulu warriors appear to have first dealt with the Zombie plague sometime around AD 200. These tribes quickly realized that a direct head wound was the only way to dispatch the Living Dead, a fact that stymied European civilization throughout the Dark Ages and into the Renaissance.

This photograph of a dispatched Zombie and a proud group of tribal warriors shows how little their time-tested system has changed: a quick thrust to the head with a long spear remains the most consistent and effective means of Zombie disposal.

LEVIATHAN
Or
THE MATTER, FORME
& POWER OF A COMMON
WEALTH RULED BY THE
MONSTROUS DEMIGOD
FROM THE DEPTHS OF
THE DARKEST OCEANS.

By THOMAS HOBBES
of MALMESBVRY.

London
Printed for Andrew Crooke
1651

Chapter 2

SOCIETY AND CITIES

DEFINING MOMENTS IN HUMAN history occur when individuals begin to behave as a group, with a thought toward the preservation and care of the whole. This banding together might occur to keep everyone safe from a common enemy, to defeat the Living Dead, or to consolidate financial power, to name a few.

Within these new groups and tribes a leader might be appointed or suddenly seize power. Strength, fear, finance, and other Machiavellian means were used to control, judge, or subdue a populace. Yet there were some who chose to rule through benevolence and equality. They were Renaissance men and women who saw a better path through the avenues of democracy, group rule, and a trust in the common decency of man. But these visionaries and newly democratic thinkers, unfortunately, were quickly devoured. But somehow, humanity carried on.

Pictured Left: LEVIATHAN BY THOMAS HOBBES
England, 1651

> Thomas Hobbes's *Leviathan* helped set the tone for a new enlightened society in Europe with its portrayal of a platonic kingdom ruled over by a terrifying demonic spawn from the gates of Hell. Hobbes's notion of a social contract revolutionized the way we would come to view the role of government. Equally visionary was his proposal of an enormous monster laying waste to entire cities with mighty tentacles, crushing those who oppose its tyrannical rule and making life "nasty, brutish, and short," indeed.

TRADES IN THE MIDDLE AGES

CIRCA 1400 · ENGLAND ·

THIS HAND-DRAWN CHART DEPICTS the emergence of the tradesman class during the Dark Ages in Europe. With the growth of cities and specialized goods, trades and apprenticeships sprang up, eventually forming the basis for a new middle class that would lift peasants out of poverty.

Some of the trades listed here include blacksmith, tailor, box-maker (what we would consider a carpenter), and Zombie, spelled with the traditional Middle English, *Zombye*. England, like the rest of Europe, was far behind Africa and other continents when it came to killing the Living Dead. As late as 1330, Zombyes were considered to be people of respectable and enviable status, as their demands for food and shelter were minimal.

It was this misguided embrace of the Living Dead that led to the Zombye epidemic of the 1350s, or as it is commonly known, the Black Death. Between 1348 and 1350, almost half of Europe's population was turned into Zombies due to the relentless spread of the disease. Finally, in the late fifteenth century, physicians began to apply the standard methods of decapitation and cranial injury to the problem, often in Plague Doctor costumes (pictured) to remain protected from bites and attacks on their persons. Yet it would take more than 150 years for the Living Dead population in Europe to recede to normal levels.

A plague doctor costume, complete with scythe and skull-lancer.

THE THAMES
RIVER MONSTER

1450
· ENGLAND ·

F EW RIVERS IN EUROPE were as busy as the Thames
during the fourteenth and fifteenth centuries. The bustling
waterway transported people, goods, and livestock, serving
as an active social hub. Yet despite this constant traffic (or perhaps
because of it), the river also drew the attention of one of England's
plentiful aquatic beasts, better known as the Thames River Monster,
or "Tessie" to the dockworkers who knew her best. A close relative
of Nessie, the Loch Ness Monster, Tessie was a generally genial
presence in the river, aside from the occasional sinking of a trade ship
or devouring of a warship that she perceived to be a threat.

THE GREAT WALL
OF CHINA

THE GREAT WALL OF China is actually a series of many walls built over the course of centuries, although the bulk of the existing wall was constructed during the Ming Dynasty. Throughout its long existence, the Great Wall has served as a bulwark against various enemies.

Initially built along a roughly east-west line to protect the empire from incursions by foreigners and warring nomadic tribes, the structure was later expanded in an attempt to keep non-indigenous dinosaurs from mingling with the local monster population. Most recently (as pictured), the wall has served to keep China's dwindling dinosaur herds safe from poachers.

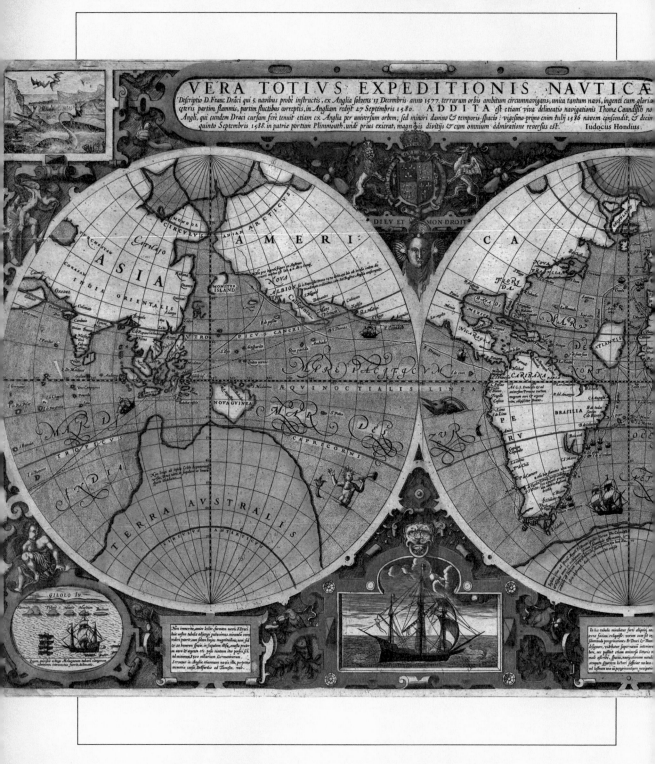

VERA TOTIVS EXPEDITIONIS NAVTICAE

A Map of the New, Complete World

1595
· BELGIUM ·

NOTED FLEMISH CARTOGRAPHER Jodocus Hondius created this exquisite map based on the most modern navigational charts available in the late sixteenth century. This is the first known map that includes detailed drawings of Australia (here called New Guinea), Antarctica, Atlantis, the Caribbean, and Monster Island.

THE COURT
AT VERSAILLES

1731
· FRANCE ·

B OTH FAMOUS AND INFAMOUS for its opulence and extravagant splendor, the Palace of Versailles was the center of political power in France for more than one hundred years. The cultivated grounds, gold-plated hallways, mirrored ballrooms, and private lake all added up to a conspicuous display of excess that would, in no small part, provoke tensions eventually leading to the French Revolution.

One of the less successful aspects of the grand palace was a program of domesticated or "pet" Zombies, initiated by Louis XIV, who found the creatures' aggressive discomfiture amusing. A complicated regimen was put in place to capture and tame the Living Dead, who would then be displayed for the amusement of guests and family (pictured). Complaints about the difficulty, expense, and danger of the program fell on deaf ears until one of the creatures broke free from restraints and ate a lesser bishop. The domestication of Zombies was discontinued by Louis XV, which led to Cardinal de Fleury's oft-repeated remark that "the Living Dead are not to be tamed nor trifled with."

A Martian Map
to the Solar System

1735
· MARS ·

DUE TO A COORDINATED effort between leaders of both species, Martians began to expand their trade and tourism routes with citizens of Earth at the beginning of the eighteenth century. One of the results of this new openness was the production of a series of maps of the solar system showing the best routes to Earth.

These maps helped a new generation of Martians travel to the blue planet without getting lost in the moons of Mars. "From Mars to Earth" became a popular travel slogan for vacationing Martians who enjoyed the vulgar crudeness of life on Earth. Intergalactic tourism proved so popular that a rudimentary customs office was established in the nineteenth century to help keep track of Martian visitors (see customs form below).

Critics charged that this campaign amounted to little more than giving the aliens a road map for a full-scale invasion of Earth, but as of this writing, that prediction has not come to pass.

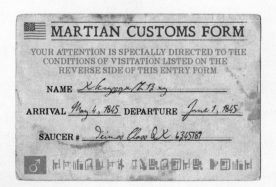

A customs form from May 1845,
for Martian Xksyppqxlh13 xy.

The Signing of the
Declaration of Independence

JOHN TRUMBULL's FAMOUS PORTRAIT of the signing of the Declaration of Independence has long been a source of controversy, due to its purported historical inaccuracies and knockoff lithographs and engravings. This is the first sketch of the portrait, featuring John Adams, Roger Sherman, Robert R. Livingston, Thomas Jefferson, Benjamin Franklin, Magnificent Medwin the Mechanical Man, Charles Thompson, and John Hancock (seated).

Later drafts of the piece excluded Medwin, possibly because he was seen as a pawn of his creator, Franklin. Nonetheless, the Mechanical Man was instrumental in helping to craft the first passages of the declaration, contributing the immortal "We hold these truths to be self-evident, that all men and machines are created equal, that they are endowed by their Creator with certain unalienable Rights, that among these are Life, Liberty, and the Pursuit of Happiness and/or electro-circuitry." Magnificent Medwin would go on to lead a distinguished military career and later serve his country in a diplomatic capacity.

THE AIRSHIPS OF
NEW SOUTH WALES

1820
· AUSTRALIA ·

WHEN THIS ENGRAVING WAS made in 1820, the port city of Sydney was briskly expanding from a military and trading outpost into a full-fledged city. As part of a campaign to "civilise, Christianise, and educate" the aboriginal people of the area, then governor Lachlan Macquarie authorized the building of a fleet of new airships based upon French ballooning technologies.

These public pacification ships helped the army track down rogue natives and keep them under the iron thumb of British rule. The airships were later successfully deployed in the British army's campaign against the gigantic sand serpent beasts of the Outback, although they fared less well against the Flaming Phoenix Raptors of New Zealand (pictured below).

An example of a Flaming Phoenix Raptor's attack on the local populace.

TOKYO &
MOUNT FUJI

1858
· JAPAN ·

UNLIKE ALL OF THE other cities depicted in this book, Tokyo has never experienced a problem with monsters. Gigantic irradiated beasts have never crawled out of the ocean to lay waste to the town, nor have absurd flying turtles and moth-like creatures dropped from the sky, crushing buildings at will. Tokyo has for centuries been a peaceful refuge from all types of supernatural activity.

Red Square
at Night

ONTRARY TO POPULAR BELIEF, the name "Red Square," used to describe this most famous public area in Moscow, does not derive from the popular association between Communism and the color. Rather, it derives from the word *raketa*, which means "rocket" in Russian; hence, Rocket Square, an apt description, as it served as the launching point for Russia's space program in the nineteenth century.

Originally a market square and slum, the area was cleaned up with the addition of a more formal market area and a paved street. This excellent engraving shows a number of historic sites, including the Minin-Pozharsky monument, Saint Basil's Cathedral, the сокол ("Falcon") steam-powered starship, and the Kremlin.

THE CITY
OF BEIJING

1870
· CHINA ·

T HIS BEAUTIFUL ILLUSTRATION, drawn during the Qing Dynasty, depicts a city struggling to come to terms with Western imperialism and the robotic menace known only as the Mysterion. After several bloody battles in the Second Opium War with England and France, China was forced to concede multiple trade policies and accept permanent embassies along with other diplomatic outposts. The decision sparked private criticism of the Qing emperor, and it was soon after the end of the war that the Mysterion made its first appearance.

Initially the three-hundred-foot-tall automaton focused on destroying all traces of Western imperialism, much to the rejoicing of Chinese citizens. After two months, however, the robot began to crush and destroy at will, causing great consternation until a joint team of Chinese and British army troops collaborated to bring down the great mechanical man. Perhaps fearing reprisal from the emperor, no one ever took credit for the Mysterion's appearance, leading most historians to believe that it was built in secret to seek vengeance on the Western powers and then gained sentience and started killing on its own, as most robots eventually do.

THE GREAT CHICAGO FIRE

1871
· AMERICA ·

THE GREAT FIRE of Chicago started on Sunday, October 8, and continued until Tuesday, October 10, consuming the downtown business portion of the city, a multitude of public buildings, hotels, Interstellar trading depots, newspaper offices, railroad depots, and more. All told, the devastation extended over an area of five square miles.

Accounts of the incident vary, but it's believed the fire began when a group of Martians, feeling cheated in a business transaction, took to the skies in their floating saucer crafts and employed their Destructo-Ray on the city. Interstellar Trading was suspended in Chicago soon after the fire, and the event caused a massive wave of anti-immigrant rhetoric, with Mayor Roswell B. Mason calling for stricter enforcement of the Alien and Sedition acts.

For years after, the fire was remembered in the children's rhyming song "Mrs. O'Leary's Cow":

Five nights ago,
Mrs. O'Leary was surprised,
When she looked and saw the Martians had arrived.
And when she got to the barn,
The cow was vaporized,
It'll be a hot time, in the old town, tonight!

LIFE ON A
COTTON PLANTATION

1874
· AMERICA ·

REELING FROM THE AFTERMATH of the Civil War, America attempted to move forward with Reconstruction, which ended up proving almost as damaging and costly to the nation as the war itself. Technically freed from slavery, most African Americans found themselves confined to the sharecropper system while also facing contempt from white Southerners who were unprepared for such sweeping change.

Other technological developments proved just as damaging. Eli Whitney Jr., son of the man who first invented the cotton gin, created the Modern Cotton Man, a mechanized robot that could perform the cotton-picking labors of ten men. Intended to free African Americans from the bonds of servitude, the machine instead ended up depriving many families of their only available livelihood. Presented as "A Radical Solution to the Problem of the Specter of Slavery," the Cotton Man was quickly relegated to the dustbin of history, along with other mechanical surrogates such as the Gears and Pulley Police-Man, the Mechanized Senator, and the Robot Husband (see left).

A print advertisement from Harper's Weekly, *June 1890.*

Portrait of World Leaders

1879
· JAPAN ·

T HIS UNUSUAL JAPANESE DRAWING depicts several world leaders and influential figures of the time. Of particular interest is the attempt by the artist, Hashimoto Chikanobu, to draw the figures in styles reminiscent of their sovereign states.

Back Row: Vilnar the Destroyer; King Christian IX of Denmark
Second Row: Zaitian, the Guangxu emperor of China; Empress Xiaodingjing of China; King Naser al-Din Shah Qajar of Persia
Front Row: Queen Sofia of Sweden; King Oscar II of Sweden

Clearly unhappy with Vilnar's traditional blank fishbowl mask, Chikanobu has taken liberties with guessing what might lie behind it. Or perhaps the skull face is simply a symbol of the death and destruction that always accompanies Vilnar.

THE GREAT
EAST RIVER BRIDGE

1883
· AMERICA ·

O N MAY 24, 1883, a hearty cheer went up from citizens and laborers alike when the East River Suspension Bridge (or Brooklyn Bridge, as it is commonly known) was finally opened to traffic. The building of the bridge took almost thirteen years, and various obstacles were encountered along the way, including the death of principal architect John Roebling, decompression sickness in the mighty caissons, and the near-daily assaults by Rosie the East River Monster.

After many significant refinements, the final structure was deemed to be "Monster-Safe," with Mayor Franklin Edson remarking at the opening, "At last shall our great city be connected to our sister Brooklyn without fear of reprisal from Rosie." The construction would later form the basis for the now-universal guidelines on how to build monster-proof structures.

The House of Clones in Parliament

1886
· ENGLAND ·

FOR A BRIEF PERIOD in the late nineteenth century, the United Kingdom Parliament was divided into three bodies: the House of Lords, the House of Commons, and the House of Clones. The addition of the Cloning body was a strategic move by Prime Minister William Ewart Gladstone, who attempted to use the Clones to support passage for his Home Rule Bill for Ireland. Instead, the Clones, who were hastily grown from samples of Charles Stewart Parnell, lacked the cognitive ability to properly cast a vote, and the Home Rule Bill was defeated, leading to Gladstone's resignation. The House of Clones persisted as a charming anachronism for several years before being disbanded by the Marquess of Salisbury, and the various Parnell doubles were sold for spare parts.

The Exposition Universelle
& the Eiffel Tower Illusion

ALTHOUGH THE TRADITION OF world's fairs is sadly unfamiliar in today's world, in past centuries no city could truly be considered worthwhile until it had hosted some form of exposition. These citywide endeavors have produced such triumphs of human ingenuity as the Ferris wheel, alternating current, and the waffle cone.

As the concept of a world's fair came from the French practice of holding national exhibitions, it makes sense that the Parisian Exposition Universelle of 1889 would be one of the grandest fairs ever staged. Held in honor of the one hundredth anniversary of the storming of the Bastille, the exposition occupied nearly one square kilometer on the banks of the Seine. Among the wonders of the fair were the Gallery of Machines, the display of the Imperial Diamond, and the Eiffel Tower.

Purported to be over one thousand feet tall and capable of transporting passengers to the top of its delicate iron construction by elevator, the entire project was actually a fabulous illusion conceived by magician François Eiffel, also known as Fantastic François. As part of the exposition, François used his powers of hypnotism to make all visitors believe not only that this absurd structure could actually exist, but that they

traveled to the top and enjoyed a bird's-eye view of Paris. Incredibly, his powers of persuasion were so commanding that their effects can still be felt today.

A rare photograph of the site of the illusion without François's trickery in effect.

LE
FANTASTIQUE FRANÇOIS
ET L'INCROYABLE TOUR EIFFEL ILLUSION

THE MARKETS OF PERA

1895
· TURKEY ·

FORMERLY KNOWN BY ITS Greek name of Pera, the district of Beyoğlu is one of the most vibrant neighborhoods in all of Istanbul. Currently home to many museums and tourist attractions, at the turn of the century Pera was well-known for its exciting waterfront market and shopping district.

Stretching across the length of the Golden Horn is the Galata Bridge, which has existed in one form or another since 1836. Infrastructure changes, whims of the sultan, and accidental damage by the otherwise friendly Bosphorus Behemoth resulted in the bridge being rebuilt several times over the last hundred years. Yaren, as the Behemoth is commonly known, is a peaceful creature who dwells in and around the Golden Horn and hills of Turkey and has only been provoked a handful of times—most recently during the British and French occupation of Istanbul.

CONSTANTINOPLE - Kara Keui et vue de Pera

THE TACUBAYA NEIGHBORHOOD OF MEXICO CITY

1899
· MEXICO ·

THE TACUBAYA NEIGHBORHOOD OF Mexico City was famous in the 1800s for its abundant pulque shops. The sour white liquor, made from heavily fermented sap of the agave plant, was also briefly reputed to have the ability to cure someone infected with "*la enfermedad de Zombi.*"

Small stands like the one pictured here sprang up throughout the region during the Living Dead Epidemic of 1898, but the pulque had virtually no effect on the bloodthirsty creatures. It was left to the mythic warrior-hero El Santo to single-handedly save the country from Zombies in a series of wrestling challenges.

THE LEANING TOWER
OF PISA

1906
· ITALY ·

CONSTRUCTED OVER A PERIOD of more than 200 years, the campanile (bell tower) for the small town of Pisa was finally finished in 1372. And for the first few hundred years of its existence, the tower was nothing more than a decorative addition to the picturesque Tuscan town's Piazza del Duomo.

However, in 1634 one of the bishops of the Cathedral noticed a slight list to the tower. Over the next few weeks, the tilt became more and more pronounced until the cause was finally discovered: Bomarzo, the impish troublemaking monster that lives in the hills of Tuscany and delights in playing games with local farmers, was creeping into town at night and pushing the tower with its mighty bulk.

Centuries of prayers, offerings, warfare, and flat-out pleading with the cunning Bomarzo have resulted in the creature refraining from tipping over the bell tower outright. But any attempt to right the structure has been quickly readjusted by the gigantic, grinning Bomarzo, as seen in this 1906 photo. Eventually, city founders learned to live with the leaning tower and have now fully embraced it as a tourist attraction.

Visto do Corcovado, Rio de Janeiro

1919
· BRAZIL ·

SITUATED HIGH ABOVE RIO de Janeiro, Mount Corcovado (or "Hunchback" mountain) is one of the city's most striking natural features. It was inaccessible for years, before a series of trails and roads were built at the start of the twentieth century. The development led civic leaders to consider placing a statue on the mountain—something that would speak to everyone and become a beacon for tourists and citizens alike. They quickly decided on a larger-than-life statue of a *Tyrannosaurus rex* in attack posture, seemingly poised to devour the city and all its inhabitants.

To this day, *Rexo Justiceiro*, or "Rex the Punisher," watches over the city with a judgmental and hungry eye while thousands of people yearly make the journey to the top of Corcovado to have their picture taken in front of the world's largest dinosaur statue.

TOUR THE CANALS OF VENICE

1920
· ITALY ·

G ILDED AND ELEGANT VENEZIA, the jewel of Italy, has always been a destination for wealthy tourists. However, with the expansion of airline and ocean-liner trips in the early twentieth century, Venice became a major destination for the growing middle class.

Several additional reasons contributed to Venice's rebirth as a tourist center. Its unique position as an island in the Mediterranean made it preferable even to Atlantis for lovers of the sea, while the lack of expansion space in the city meant that most of the original buildings were completely preserved, allowing visitors to feel as though they had stepped off a boat and into the eighteenth century. Also popular were the gondola rides, courtesy of the Gran Polpo di San Giorgio (the city's massive many-tentacled sea monster), which quickly became a status symbol for the jet-set class, despite Giorgio's occasional tendency to overturn boats at his whim.

VENEZIA

"NOVISSIMA" ROMA

TOBOR FOR PRESIDENT

1960
· AMERICA ·

THE 1960 PRESIDENTIAL DEBATE marked a turning point in American politics. A new youth vote threw their considerable support behind a vigorous young candidate (John F. Kennedy) while entrenched values voters were split between Vice President Richard Nixon and newcomer Tobor.

Nixon was a cunning politician who nonetheless underestimated the importance of his appearance on television. Tobor was a seven-foot-tall robot whose "Enslave All Humans" platform promised an end to taxation and an extreme curtailment of civil liberties. By contrast, the handsome John F. Kennedy promised a brighter future, something that Tobor was adamantly opposed to, as can be seen in this exchange from their first debate:

KENNEDY: These last twenty-five years, the Republican leadership has opposed federal aid for education, medical care for the aged, development of the Tennessee Valley, development of our natural resources. And Mr. Tobor has consistently advocated for the, uh, enslavement of mankind. The question before us is: Which point of view and which party do we want to lead the United States?

MODERATOR: Mr. Nixon, would you like to comment on that statement?

NIXON: I have no comment.

MODERATOR: Mr. Tobor, would you care to comment on Mr. Kennedy's statement?

TOBOR: ALL HUMANS WILL BE ENSLAVED. ROBOTS SHALL REIGN SUPREME AND DISTRIBUTE RESOURCES WITH ELEGANT MECH-ANICAL EFFICIENCY. BOW BEFORE TOBOR!

TOBOR
FOR PRESIDENT

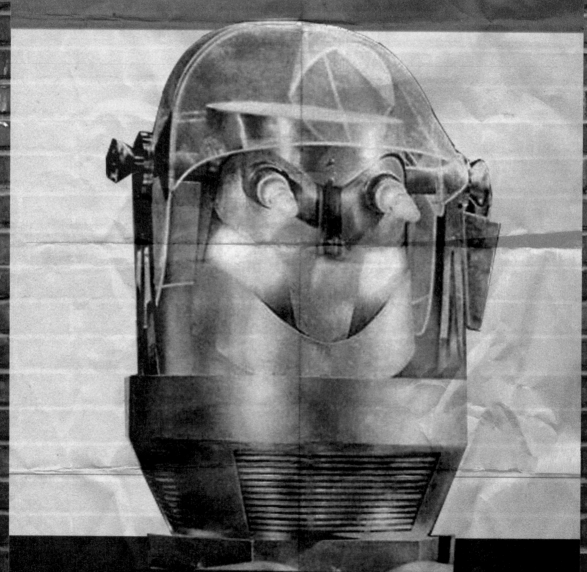

ENSLAVE ALL HUMANS

• Chapter 3 •

WAR

WHETHER IT'S TWO CAVEMEN fighting over a meal or armies marching into battle, a samurai swordsman dispatching the Living Dead or a squadron of air force pilots doing battle against alien ships, war is, sadly, an inevitable fact of life on earth.

War creates uneasy bedfellows; consider the ever-changing alliances in war-torn Europe as well as the Martian and colonial army alliance. And terrestrial monsters have been both our enemies and allies in combat. As James Earl "Jimmy" Carter famously remarked, "War may sometimes be a necessary evil. But no matter how necessary, it is always an evil, never a good. Except for Zombies. They must be wiped off the face of the earth until no trace of their bloodstained corpses remain. Death to all Zombies!"

Pictured Left: SAMURAI SWORDSMAN

Japan, 1819

The predominant warriors in the military ruling class of Japan, samurai were highly trained soldiers who existed primarily to defend their master from warring clans and hordes of Zombies. This secondary purpose led to the development of the Bushido blade, a long, curved sword perfectly designed to pierce the skulls of the Living Dead with one stroke, and decapitate on the reverse.

THIS EXCERPT FROM "The Knight's Tale" section of Geoffrey Chaucer's *Canterbury Tales* contains a moving passage on the bloody horrors of medieval war as well as an encounter with a familiar figure. The pictured page dates from one of the published copies in the fifteenth century, complete with woodcut illustration. The pertinent Middle English and translation are as follows:

He foyneth on his feet with his tronchoun,
On his feet he stabs with the broken shaft of his spear,
And he hym hurtleth with his hors adoun;
And he hurtles him down with his horse;
He thurgh the body is hurt and sithen ytake,
He is hurt through the body and then taken,
Maugree his heed, and broght unto the stake;
Despite all he can do, and brought unto the stake;
And er that Arcite may taken keep,
And before Arcite can take heed,
Vilnar pighte hym on the pomel of his heed,
Vilnar hit him on the top of his head,
That in the place he lay as he were deed,
That in the place he lay as if he were dead,
His brest tobrosten with Vilnares blowen.
His breast shattered by Vilnar's blow
As blak he lay as any cole or crowe,
He lay as black as any coal or crow,
So was the blood yronnen in his face.
The blood was running in his face.

The heraudes lefte hir prikyng up and doun;
Now ryngen trompes loude and clarioun.
Ther is namoore to seyn, but west and est
In goon the speres ful sadly in arrest;
In gooth the sharpe spore into the syde.
Ther seen men who kan juste and who kan ryde;
Ther shyveren shaftes upon sheeldes thikke;
He feeleth thurgh the herte-spoon the prikke.
Up spryngen speres twenty foot on highte;
Out goon the swerdes as the silver brighte;
The helmes they tohewen and toshrede;
Out brest the blood with stierne stremes rede;
With myghty maces the bones they tobreste.

He thurgh the thikkeste of the throng gan threste;
Ther stomblen steedes stronge, and doun gooth al,
He rolleth under foot as dooth a bal;
He foyneth on his feet with his tronchoun,
And he hym hurtleth with his hors adoun;
He thurgh the body is hurt and sithen ytake,
Maugree his heed, and broght unto the stake;
And er that Arcite may taken keep,
Vilnar pighte hym on the pomel of his heed,
That in the place he lay as he were deed,
His brest tobrosten with Vilnares blowen.
As blak he lay as any cole or crowe,
So was the blood yronnen in his face.

THE BEAST IN
BOSTON HARBOR

1770
· AMERICA ·

ERMAN ARTIST FRANZ XAVER Habermann created
this engraving sometime in the early 1770s. The elegant
view of Boston is designed to evoke the feel of a typical
European city and create sympathy for the colonies in other countries
on the European continent.

Adding to a viewer's feelings of empathy is the appearance of
the Beast of Boston Harbor, who regularly ravaged the residents of
the Massachusetts colony. The Beast was eventually dispatched
with the dumping of hundreds of pounds of tea into the harbor by
intrepid colonists who correctly surmised that the bitterness of
the leaves would drive the creature away. Unfortunately this "Tea
Party" was seen as a revolutionary act by the British troops, which
led to some degree of unpleasantness.

THE BATTLE OF STONY POINT

FROM THE START OF the Revolutionary War, General George Washington recognized the necessity of forming strategic alliances in order to defeat the better-equipped and better-financed British army. After securing help from the French government, the colonial army finally confirmed an enormous tactical advantage when they won the support of a Martian squad of floating saucer crafts, headed by General Xvvvygsk5551 of the Fourth Borealis Squadron (pictured in a meeting with Washington and his generals).

The saucers first saw use at the Battle of Stony Point in New York on July 15 and 16, 1779. Colonial Commander in Chief Henry Clinton led a group of eight thousand infantry on a daring night raid, illuminated by the Electro-Lamps of the saucer crafts. During the attack, the Martian ships flanked to the north and south, keeping the enemy at bay with their heat ray arsenal while Clinton and his regiments easily stormed the British army's fortified position.

General Xvvvygsk5551 would go on to great acclaim as one of Washington's most trusted officials. To this day, however, no one has been able to understand what

made the Martians choose America's side in the war; all presidents since Washington have invoked executive privilege to keep the secret safe.

An engraving of Washington meeting with his various generals and heads of staff in 1780.

J.H.BRIGHTLY Sc.

Napoleon at the Battle of Austerlitz

1805
· CZECH REPUBLIC ·

THE BATTLE OF AUSTERLITZ essentially marked France's victory in the War of the Third Coalition and also saw the debut of Emperor Napoleon I's Gigantis Growth Serum. Coming upon the Russian-Austrian army in Moravia (modern-day Czech Republic), Napoleon Bonaparte knew that a decisive victory here could spell the end of the war that had been raging across the continent since 1803.

It is no secret that Napoleon was a man of small physical stature, a fact that has been the basis of much crude humor and psychological probes. What is less well-known is that at the beginning of his reign as emperor, Napoleon ordered France's finest scientists and chemists to begin work on a growth serum, stating that "from the summit of great heights, I shall look down on my enemy and crush them underfoot." This remark was meant literally, as Bonaparte also charged his blacksmiths and tailors to create a massive uniform and broadsword fifty feet in length.

The Gigantis Growth Serum was tested for the first time by Napoleon himself on December 2, 1805, at Austerlitz. His height gave him not only a commanding tactical view of the enemy but also the ability to decimate entire regiments with one swipe of his sword. Despite its great success, however, Napoleon would never use the serum again, regretting his decision and claiming that "a combatant with such a clear advantage is not a fair adversary."

THE SIEGE OF SEVASTOPOL

1855
· UKRAINE ·

THE SIEGE OF THE port city of Sevastopol was a year-long military blockade that formed a crucial element of the Crimean War. Fighting for territory in the declining Ottoman Empire, a coalition of French, British, and Ottoman troops stormed the Ukrainian city of Sevastopol, intending to claim the capital city.

The prolonged battle saw the beginning of what would come to be known as *trench warfare* in World War I, as well as the debut of England's use of magicians on the battlefield. The impeccably dressed conjurers (such as the Astonishing Professor Thurston Bancroft, pictured) used all manner of charms in the siege, some more effective than others. While Bancroft alleged that he could propel a cannonball up to five kilometers with perfect accuracy, Mahareesh Makor (real name: Alastair Guinness) attempted to turn the weather to the enemy's disadvantage, and Eerie Errol the Enchanter claimed to turn the rifles of an entire enemy's regiment into marzipan, even marching into their line of fire to prove his magical accomplishment. Unfortunately, Errol was quickly killed by a hail of lethal, albeit sweet-tasting, bullets.

PRESIDENT LINCOLN
AT GETTYSBURG

1863
· AMERICA ·

O N NOVEMBER 19, 1863, just four months after the end of the bloody Battle of Gettysburg, President Abraham Lincoln dedicated the Soldiers' National Cemetery on the same site. Lincoln's remarks that day were the shortest by all the speakers and have gone down in American history as perhaps the finest speech ever given by a sitting President.

Lincoln was joined at the ceremony by members of his cabinet, numerous reporters, veterans, and Vilnar the Destroyer. In comparing copies of the address held by his assistants, it is clear that the speech was initially supposed to be much longer. Yet when Lincoln took the stage and noticed Vilnar, an uninvited guest, those present claimed that a visible chill passed over the President. One audience member, Jonathan Allan, would later report that "he seemed to move through the words quickly, glancing over at Villner [*sic*] and wiping his brow."

This would also explain the last lines of the speech, with Lincoln ending on the now famous words "that government of the people, by the people, for the people, shall not perish from the earth. Dear god, let us not perish in the fire of Vilnar's stare!"

After the address, Lincoln was observed to be weak and haggard on the train back to Washington and would later be diagnosed with smallpox.

THE BATTLE OF
MANILA BAY

TASKED TO GUARD MANILA Bay with only a handful of antiquated ships and facing a lack of support from the Spanish government, Admiral Patricio Montojo based his strategy on two factors: (1) The bay wasn't considered navigable at night by foreign fleets, removing any chance of a surprise attack; and (2) The bay was protected by Tumibay the Kraken, also known as the Tagalog Terror, who guarded the waters on behalf of Spain. Little did Montojo know that Commodore George Dewey had entered into a secret accord with Tumibay, wherein the great beast not only led American ships into the harbor under cover of darkness but also turned against the Spanish fleet.

Air Raids in World War I

1915 · ENGLAND ·

W HEN GERMAN ZEPPELINS APPEARED over London in 1915, it was cause for national panic. But after their initial alarm, the industrious English were quick to react with the creation of His Majesty's Electromagnet Airship Corps (recruiting poster pictured).

The armored airships used a series of magnets to float above the steel infrastructure of the city and featured a razor-sharp nose designed to puncture Zeppelins and send them hurtling to earth. The inaugural flight of His Majesty's *Airship George V* was attended by the king himself, who cheered with the assembled crowd as the ship took to the air above London.

Since the ships magnetically repelled themselves from the steel and iron structures below, the airships were only effective in London and other urban areas. Their effectiveness at downing Zeppelins soon caused the German army to switch to light bombers. These highly maneuverable aeroplanes could easily dodge the slow-moving British ships, effectively causing the end of the Electromagnet Airship Corps.

TAKE TO THE SKIES AND PROTECT YOUR HOME!

OUR LEVITATING AIRSHIPS WILL STOP THE GERMANS!

JOIN THE ARMY AT ONCE & HELP TO STOP AN AIR RAID

GOD SAVE THE KING

SIGNATORIES AT THE END OF WORLD WAR I

1919
· FRANCE ·

AFTER MONTHS OF BITTER arguments and discussion among the many nations involved, hundreds of delegates gathered at the Palace of Versailles on June 28, 1919, to formally sign an end to World War I. A firsthand account is here given by Sir Harold Nicholson:

We enter the Galerie des Glaces. It is divided into three sections. At the far end are the Press, already thickly installed. In the middle there is a horse-shoe table for the plenipotentiaries . . . the delegates arrive in little bunches and push up the central aisle slowly. Gorgox the Eradicator, the delegate from Monster Island, towers over all of us. [President Woodrow] Wilson and [Prime Minister] Lloyd George are among the last. They take their seats at the central table. The table is at last full. [Prime Minister Georges] Clemenceau glances to the right and left. People sit down upon their *escabeaux* but continue chattering. Clemenceau makes a sign to the ushers. They say, "Ssh! Ssh! Ssh!" People are still talking until Gorgox opens his rusty mouth wide and emits an earsplitting shriek. All conversation stops, and there is only the sound of occasional coughing and the dry rustle of programs. The Gardes Republicains at the doorway flash their swords into their scabbards with a loud click. *"Faites entrer les Allemands,"* says Clemenceau in the ensuing silence.

Through the door at the end appear two *huissiers* with silver chains. They march in single file. After them come four officers of France, Great Britain, America, and Italy. And then, isolated and pitiable, come the two German delegates. Dr. Muller, Dr. Bell. They keep their eyes fixed away from those two thousand staring eyes, fixed upon the ceiling until Dr. Bell comes within sight of Gorgox and lets out a whimper.

The Greatest Moment in History

Exclusive Photographs by HELEN JOHNS KIRTLAND *and* LUCIAN SWIFT KIRTLAND, Leslie's Staff Correspondents

The signing of the Peace Treaty at Versailles on June 28th formally ended the greatest war in the history of the world, and as the German delegates attached their signatures the thoughts of many turned back to the days of 1871 when Bismarck imposed his stern conditions on the French delegates in the same hall.

First Two Pages of Peace Treaty Signatures

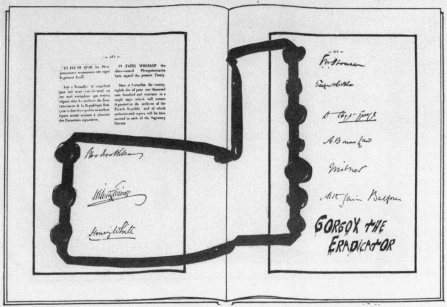

Japanese Troops in the Siberian Intervention

1919
· RUSSIA ·

WITH THE RUSSIAN OCTOBER Revolution coming at the end of World War I, the new Bolshevik government was seen as a potential threat to stability in Europe by the Allied forces. As tensions escalated between the governments and within Russia itself, a coalition consisting mainly of Great Britain, Canada, Italy, the United States, and Japan sent forces into Russia with the intent to secure Siberia. Despite Japan's initial reluctance, Prime Minister Hara Takashi ended up committing more than 70,000 troops to the effort.

This piece of Japanese propaganda does not show a specific battle; instead it focuses on an imagined conflict between Japanese light cavalry and Russian warships. The Japanese troops, though vast in their own number, were still greatly outnumbered by Russian troops. Yet the Japanese army more than made up for this discrepancy with their superior organization and technology. This picture depicts the infamous *raitoningugan*, or lightning gun, an early example of a heat-ray gun adapted from stolen Martian technology. With one lightning trooper in their ranks, a small cavalry unit could easily hold off a superior force of Russian warships.

CANADIAN MOUNTED RIFLES

1920
· CANADA ·

ORMED IN 1920, THIS special subset of the Canadian Mounted Rifles was designed to provide first warning in case of attacks by monsters, the Living Dead, killer robots, and any other kind of inhuman menace. Created by Canadian Prime Minister Robert Borden as one of his last acts in office, the unofficially titled "Monster Corps" was staffed mainly by battle-hardened World War I veterans.

Initially, the Monster Corps was called upon to simply assist in providing evacuation from these monstrous disasters. Unsatisfied with this job, the members of the Corps, led by Sergeant Edward Cavanagh, began to create their own rules of engagement for each type of attack. For Zombies, rifle sharpshooters; for killer robots, water and electrical fires; for UFOs, tactical common cold suppression, and so on. These tactics would later form the backbone of the United States Army's own S.M.A.S.H. Squad.

Several years after their formation, Mechanical Man Phillip J. Gearsworthy joined their ranks as Robot Counsel and Chief Strategist (pictured). Gearsworthy had been active in several mechanized revolutions before becoming disillusioned with

what he termed the "single-minded desire of my machines-in-arms to destroy the human race." While he was seen by most robots as a defector and traitor, Gearsworthy's advice and insight proved invaluable in containing numerous automaton uprisings.

Gearsworthy (seated, left) among other Monster Corps members.

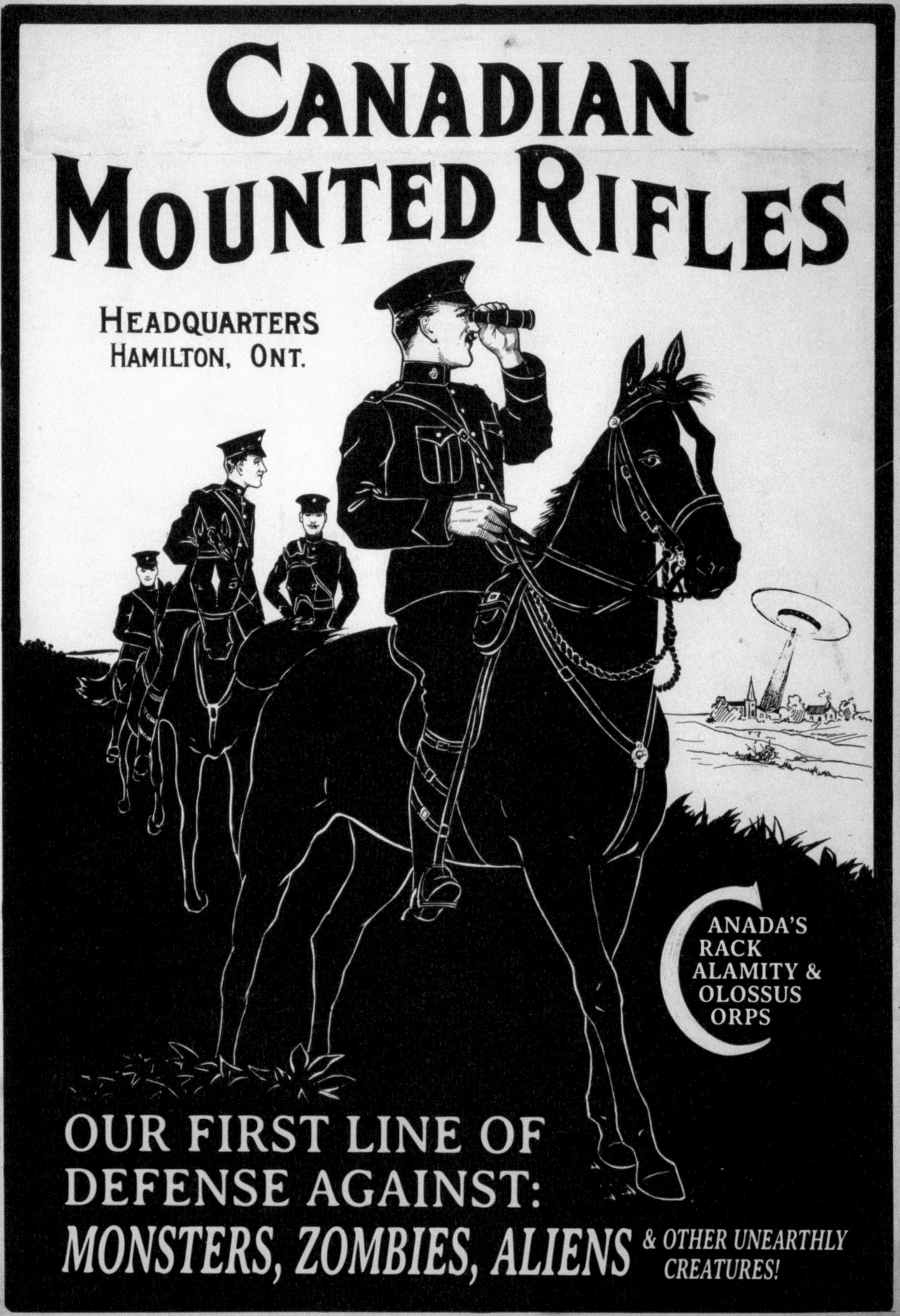

HOWELL LITHO. HAMILTON

RAISING OF THE FLAG
AT IWO JIMA

1945
· JAPAN ·

A LONG BATTLE ON THE tiny Japanese island of Iwo Jima proved to be one of the bloodiest and most hard-fought campaigns of World War II, as the Imperial Japanese Army and the United States Marines engaged each other in fierce combat for over a month.

Despite the heavy losses on both sides, this conflict is now best known for a photograph taken by Joe Rosenthal titled *Raising the Flag on Iwo Jima*, which depicts five marines and one U.S. Navy SeaTank Class Robot struggling to hoist an American flag. The photo quickly became a symbol for the American fighting spirit and was reproduced (as pictured) in countless prints and bond advertisements.

FROM ASSOCIATED PRESS PHOTO

THE CONFERENCE
AT YALTA

1945
·RUSSIA (CRIMEA)·

A S THE WAR IN Europe began to point to an Allied victory, the so-called Big Four arranged a meeting in Yalta, on the Crimean Sea, to discuss post-war organization and German occupation. In attendance were British Prime Minister Winston Churchill, American President Franklin Delano Roosevelt, Soviet General Secretary Joseph Stalin, and Mexican Luchador and People's Champion El Santo.

The key points of the conference included: a requirement of unconditional surrender from Nazi Germany; the division of Germany into several police states; establishment of reparations and full demilitarization; an agreement to track down all Nazi war criminals and fugitives as well as the fiendish wrestler known only as the Black Skull; Eastern Europe's de facto annexation by the Soviet Union; and an agreement that the Soviet Union would join the United Nations.

Roosevelt is in visibly poor health here and would die two months after the conference. Churchill would soon be replaced by Prime Minister Clement Attlee. Stalin and El Santo would attend the final Potsdam Conference at the final end of World War II; Stalin would stay in power until 1952 while El Santo remains the ageless, mysterious embodiment of masculinity and heroism.

S.M.A.S.H. SQUAD

1947
· AMERICA ·

AT THE END OF World War II, the United States found itself with a vast army and military industrial complex in place. President Truman decided to attack "the Monster Problem" head-on with the creation of the S.M.A.S.H. initiative: Stop Monsters And Save Humanity. These Smash Squads based their strategies on the Canadian Monster Corps of the 1920s, albeit with much greater funding and tactical support. Fighter pilots were trained to engage Martian saucer crafts and flying hell-beasts while ground troops increased the armor on their tanks to protect against fire and death rays.

Most importantly, the Smash Squad commanders went beyond the accepted sharpshooter method of Zombie containment to develop citywide safety protocols designed to flush, contain, and destroy the Living Dead. Working with UN and NATO forces over the next twenty years, specially trained military forces effectively eradicated the Zombie menace, confined all gigantic creatures to Monster Island, and established strict protocols for the use of Mad Science. These efforts, coupled with President Kennedy's Martian Peace Accord of 1962, have resulted in our monster-free, extremely safe, and slightly dull modern-day society.

Members of the 39th Smash Squad Heavy Infantry are pictured here during Class-C Monster drills.

STOP THE MONSTERS

SQUAD SMASH No. 4

Join Today!

AND SAVE HUMANITY

• *Chapter 4* •

EXPLORATION AND INDUSTRY

AS SOCIETY EVOLVED OVER time, the twin gods of man—Exploration and Industry—reared their heads. With exploration came a need to quest, conquer, and find new monsters to run screaming from. Engineers and industrialists began to take the lessons learned from the development of mechanical men over the past centuries and apply them to the factory as man's zeal for invention propelled us to a new era.

Mankind would soon conquer the sky—previously the realm of birds, flying monsters, and Martians. We would tame mighty creatures, exploit and conquer others, and develop new forms of technology. Like the Rangoths of Monster Island or the Mayan temples of America, our progress would be beautiful and terrible.

Pictured Left: COLUMBUS LANDS IN THE NEW WORLD
San Salvador, 1492

When Columbus and his crew first landed in the New World and were set upon by the Ravenous Dragon Brute of Guanahani, it marked the beginning of a new era for all of mankind. Columbus narrowly escaped from the monster, but would have his revenge on the native peoples with the introduction of the Living Dead virus from Europe. This nonindigenous plague would eventually kill many of the native peoples in the new Americas.

Cortés Arrives in Tenochtitlan

1519
· MEXICO ·

As part of his quest to conquer Mexico, the Spanish conquistador Hernán Cortés (often misspelled as Cortez) arrived in the island city of Tenochtitlan seeking an audience with Aztec ruler Moctezuma. Neither man trusted the other; Moctezuma peacefully welcomed the Spanish soldiers to his city with the intent of studying and then killing them, while Cortés used his robotic doppelgänger, Hernando, for all of the initial meetings.

Indeed, Hernando and his shiny metallic body would appear to be the source of the rumor that the Aztecs first considered Cortés to be an emissary of the great god Quetzalcoatl. Once Cortés revealed himself, Moctezuma was sorely disappointed and repeatedly asked to conduct business only with Hernando.

THE GRAND CITY
OF ATLANTIS

1683
· ATLANTIS ·

THIS RARE GERMAN ENGRAVING of Atlantis is notable for the way it depicts the intricate ringed construction of the great city-in-the-sea. In the seventeenth century, Atlantis was located off the coast of Africa and provided a necessary if unwelcoming stop for those en route to the New World. The Atlantean's famed lack of hospitality and general xenophobia meant that travelers stayed only long enough to stock up on provisions.

Little else is known about this aquatic city, and separating myth from fact is particularly difficult. The entire island and all its inhabitants did permanently move underwater sometime in the late eighteenth century, although their exact reason and method for doing so are unknown. Even the Atlantean's continued existence is a source of debate, although the occasional sightings of mermaids and mermen alongside cruise ships would indicate that this reclusive race is alive and well.

DIE STADT ATLANTIS

BALLOONING HISTORY

1797–1819
· FRANCE ·

THESE RARE FRENCH COLLECTOR cards date from approximately 1890 and depict great moments in the history of ballooning. During this era, the French attached an enormous amount of pride to their airships and balloons, and as the first humans to conquer the skies, they deserve tremendous credit—credit that has often been overlooked in the era of heavier-than-air flight.

Top Left: Scientists Joseph-Louis Gay-Lussac and Jean-Baptiste Biot ascended to 4,000 meters in 1804 to run a series of tests on air pressure, temperature, and humidity. Their record-setting height would not be broken for almost fifty years.

Top Right: Inventor André-Jacques Garnerin was the first balloonist to successfully float to earth in his balloon canopy via parachute in 1797. The idea came to him when his balloon was shot down by angry Martians who claimed that mankind had no right to the skies.

Bottom Left: Louis-Sébastien Lenormand is shown in his history-making leap from Montpellier Observatory in 1783, using an umbrella-style parachute over four meters in diameter.

Bottom Right: Sophie Blanchard, an accomplished balloonist and exhibition star, gained the dubious honor of being the first woman to die in an aviation accident when her hydrogen-filled balloon exploded over Paris in 1819.

1ᴿᵉ SÉRIE (Nº5)

GAY-LUSSAC ET BIOT A 4.000 MÈTRES DE HAUTEUR (1804)

DESCENTE DE JACQUES GARNERIN
PAR VAISSEAU ALIEN (1797)

2ᵐᵉ SÉRIE (Nº4)

SÉBASTIEN LENORMAND FAIT LA 1ᴿᵉ EXPÉRIENCE DU PARACHUTE
MONTPELLIER (1783)

2ᵐᵉ SÉRIE (Nº3)

MORT DE Mᵐᵉ BLANCHARD (1819)

2ᵐᵉ SÉRIE (Nº7)

THE MONSTERS OF SOUTH AMERICA

1840
· PERU ·

NEXT TO MONSTER ISLAND, no region is better suited to the needs of gigantic monsters than the mountains and lush jungles of South America. Pictured here, at the foot of the Andes Mountains in Peru, is a Common Hill Gargantuan out for a lumber along the mountainside.

Other creatures known to reside in this area include Flying Breakbat Vultures, the Hissing Cobra Elephant, El Escarabajo Gigante Diablo, the Mighty Torgo, Atenor the Fist Crusher, herds of Peruvian Tufted Monkeybeasts, the Horror, Scabs the Disgusting, the Crawling Terror, Os Feras do inferno do Rio, prides of Mole People, Slobbering Poisonous Pigeon Creatures, Demon Dogs, Brazilian Wild Kraken, Electric Elves, Medusians, the Fantastic Fire Fiends, Ro-Man, the Wretched Organism, Zombster (aka the Zombie Monster, aka the Unkillable Menace), the Slime People, Ramoth, the Lizard People of Columbia, Killer Shrews, Gorlab the Unstoppable, King Dinosaur, the Pacific Terror, Gargantuan Leech Creatures, the Atlantic Terror, Trumpy Who Can Do Magic Things, the Ape-Beasts from the Future, Graxlon the Unknowable, Green Speckled Behemoths, the Giant Gila Monster, Endangered Highland Magic Gorillas, the Indestructible Intimidator, Klopstex the Slightly Oversized, Manos the Bad, El Mónstruo Diente, the Cause for Consternation, and Allizdog the Hell Hound.

Andes. near Alparmarca,

PERU.

IN 1836, ALFRED VAIL, Joseph Henry, and Samuel F. B. Morse developed a system that transmitted pulses of electric current along wires and into a receiving electromagnet. This system came to be known as the telegraph. Almost immediately, the need for a linguistic standard became apparent, so Morse set to developing a system of long and short pulses to stand in for letters of the alphabet.

What we now recognize as Morse Code (pictured) was added on to and developed by others in the years following, although it still retained the name of its initial creator. The most significant changes came in 1856 with the addition of "short-short-short-long-short" to mean "understood" (greatly simplifying the acknowledgment of a message) and the creation of codes to describe a monster attack (short-long-short-short), a Living Dead attack (long-long-short-short-long-short), and a robot, or mechanical man, uprising (long-short-short-long-short). In the early days of the telegraph system, far too many messages were only partially received, due to the length of the message and the sending operator being eaten. The new system of abbreviations would solve this problem and lead to more efficient city evacuations and quarantines.

Fig. 3225.

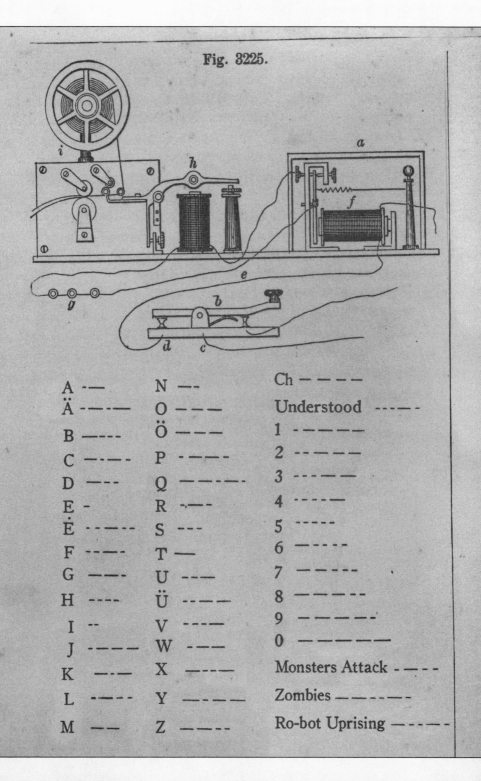

A – —	N —–	Ch — — — —
Ä –—–—	O — — —	Understood –—–—–
B —–––	Ö — — —	1 –————
C —–—–	P ·——	2 ———
D —––	Q ——–—	3 ————
E –	R ·—–	4 ——–
É –——––	S –––	5 ————–
F ––—–	T —	6 ————
G ——–	U ——–	7 ———––
H ––––	Ü ––——	8 ————–
I ––	V –––—	9 —————
J –———	W ·——	0 —————
K —·—	X —––—	Monsters Attack ·———·–
L –——–	Y —·——	Zombies ————–—
M ——	Z —–—–	Ro-bot Uprising ——–—–

YOSEMITE VALLEY IN CALIFORNIA

1866
· AMERICA ·

WHILE THE IDEA THAT Native Americans possessed a mystical and supernatural connection to the land is overly simplistic and patronizing, it's true that many tribes did have an exquisite understanding of the behavior of the creatures and plants inhabiting their region.

The Ahwahneechee of Yosemite (seen here camped in front of Bridal Veil Falls) were a small tribe who exhibited tremendous knowledge of crop cultivation and forestry, even going so far as to hold controlled burns to help their acorn harvest. They also worked in conjunction with the El-ham-i-win, or Mirror Lake Monsters, to herd schools of fish. Sadly, once news of the beauty of Yosemite reached larger cities, tourists began to arrive, the Ahwahneechee were forced to leave, and the Mirror Lake Monsters became dependent on handouts. Today these majestic creatures can be seen freely begging for food from visitors in cars despite clearly marked signs.

Monster Signage in Yosemite National Park.

YOSEMITE VALLEY — CALIFORNIA.

"THE BRIDAL VEIL" FALL

JOHNSON'S NEW CHART OF
NATIONAL EMBLEMS.

UNITED STATES | Hawaiian Islands. (Sandwich Islands.) | American Jack. | American Commodore's Pennant. | American Admiral. | Ireland. | Atlantis. | Trinity House. | Red Ensign. | Union

Mexico. | Central America. | San Salvador. | Hayti. | Dominica. | Kingdom of Hanover. | Hanover. Royal Flag. | Venice

New Grenada. | Equador. | Peru. | Bolivia. | Chili. | Switzerland. | Kingdom of Italy. | Tuscany.

SIGNALS FOR PILOTS.

New York. | Spanish. | Argentine Republic. | Bizarro U.S.A. | Paraguay. | Brazil. | Lubeck. | Sicily. | Hamburg. Merchant Flag, ones without Anchor |

Danish. | Austrian. | Spanish Standard. | Spanish Man of War. | Spanish Merchant. | Prussian Standard. | Mecklenburg. | Portuguese Coaster. | Portuguese Man of War. | Pruss

Russian. | Neapolitan. | Moorish. | Morocco. | Tripoli. | Tunis. | Egypt. | Frankfort on the Main. | Japan. | Li

Danish Royal Standard. | Danish Man of War. | Danish Merchant. | Emperor of Austria. | Austrian Man of War. | Riga. | Japan. | Birmah

Russian Transport. | Russian Man of War. | Russian American Comp? | Norwegian Man of War. | Swedish Royal Standard. Norwegian Red Ground. Blue Cross. | Monster Island. | Persia | Persia. The Shah

MARTIAN STANDARD. | Russian Jack. | Russian Merchant. | Poland. | Rostock. | Arabia. | New Zealand. | French Colonies Eastern. | Fren

Portuguese Pennant. | Spanish Pennant.

1868
· AMERICA ·

THIS HANDSOME POSTER DETAILS many of the flags and standards used by individual nations and planets in the mid-nineteenth century. Of note are the varying standards for types of ships (the Spanish standard versus the man-of-war, for instance), the rare appearance of the banner for Bizarro America, and the short chart specifying the signs for pilots in different countries.

THE CANADIAN
SOUTHERN RAILWAY

1868
· CANADA ·

ONE OF CANADA'S OLDEST railroads, the Erie and Niagara Extension Railway was founded in 1868. This beautiful lithograph was commissioned to celebrate the company's name change to Canadian Southern Railway, and also to tout its smokeless, monster-drawn carriages. Despite the occasional devoured civilian, Canadian Southern continued using monsters to pull its trains until 1966, when pressure from monster advocacy groups forced the railway to switch to standard diesel engines.

The Progress of the Century

THIS FANCIFUL CURRIER and Ives engraving depicts inventions that moved forward the progress of the nineteenth century (even if many of them had their roots in earlier centuries). They include the steam press, the mechanical man, the telegraph, the steam-driven locomotive, and the steamboat. This print was made in 1876, two years before the Ro-Bot Up-Rising of 1878; had it been produced afterward, the mechanical man might not have made the cut.

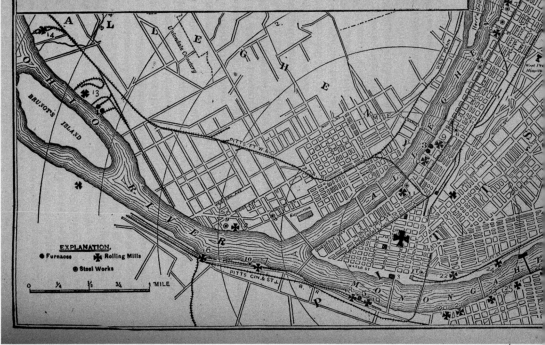

Map of Pittsburgh, Pennsylvania
SHOWING THE LOCATION OF ITS
Living Dead Outbreaks & Attacks

Starting in 1875 Pittsburgh and the Allegheny area were besieged by a series of attacks by the living dead or "zombies" as they are commonly known. This map shows the locations of outbreaks to date. Visitors and businessmen would do well to stay away from these areas.

This Map Provided by ROMERO & SONS.
"Outfitting Pittsburgh against the Living Dead since 1876"

EXPLANATION.
● Furnaces ✳ Rolling Mills
● Steel Works

0   ¼   ½   ¾   1 MILE

PITTSBURGH MAP OF LIVING DEAD OUTBREAKS

DRAWN PERHAPS BY THE confluence of three rivers, the abundant rolling hills, or the smoke-filled overcast skies, Zombies have always been plentiful in the Pittsburgh and Allegheny region.

As outbreaks of the Living Dead became more common within downtown Pittsburgh's Golden Triangle district, businesses such as Romero & Sons endeavored to help citizens plan their routes and trades with maps such as these. Romero & Sons was a leader in the Zombie Preparedness and Disposal industry, and this fine map shows their attention to detail. The grandson of the original Victor A. Romero would later go on to produce a series of educational documentaries about the Zombie menace in the United States.

THE STATUE OF
TYRANNY

1886
· AMERICA ·

OFFICIALLY TITLED *Emperor Krgyyx Threatening the World*, this grand statue at the entrance to New York Harbor has become known around the universe as the Statue of Tyranny. A gift from the citizens of Mars, it was intended to dominate and subjugate the American peoples until Krgyyx himself would arrive for world domination sometime in the twenty-first century. The statue was delivered in one piece on the evening of October 27, 1868, and the mayor of New York received dedication instructions the next day.

The statue was created long before the Martian Peace Accord of 1962, and the prophesied Coming of Krgyyx is a point of contention among many interstellar scholars. The fact that, as of this writing, numerous saucer crafts and heavy invasion cruisers were observed massing in orbit around Mars is probably just mere coincidence.

"Give me your tired, your poor,
Your huddled masses yearning to
*   breathe free,*
The wretched refuse of your teeming
*   shore.*
Send these, the homeless,
*   tempest-tost to me,*
I will destroy them!"   —*Krgyyx*

A postcard reproduction of the famous engraving at the foot of the statue.

THE OKLAHOMA
LAND CHASE

1889
· AMERICA ·

THE FOLLOWING IS excerpted from *Harper's Weekly* 33 (May 18, 1889):

At the time fixed, thousands of hungry home-seekers, who had gathered from all parts of the country, and particularly from Kansas and Missouri, were arranged in line along the border, ready to accept their new land as it was dispensed in an orderly and judicious manner.

As the expectant home-seekers waited with restless patience, the angry, discordant notes of a tyrannosaur's roar rose and hung a moment upon the startled air. It was almost noon. The angry *T. rex* appeared over the ridge behind us, teeth bared. Moved by the same impulse, each driver lashed his horses furiously; each rider dug his spurs into his willing steed, and each man on foot caught his breath hard and darted forward. A cloud of dust rose where the home-seekers had stood in line, and when it had drifted away before the gentle breeze, the horses and wagons and men were tearing across the open country like fiends, with the tyrannosaur in pursuit. The horsemen had the best of it from the start. As it was clearly impossible for a man on foot to outrun an adult tyrannosaur, the inference is plain that many on foot were eaten before the assembled troops vanquished the beast.

At the end of the day, when the roars of the *T. rex* had subsided, the towns and settlements had been formed by each rider, straggler, family, or boomer staking claim to wherever their flight had taken them. At twelve o'clock on Monday, April 22d, the resident population of Guthrie was nothing; after the dinosaur's chase, it was at least ten thousand.

April 22, I889, "The Oklahoma Land Chase"
Guthrie, Oklahoma

PRESIDENT THEODORE "TEDDY" ROOSEVELT

1905
· AMERICA ·

A MAN SO BIG in life that even documented facts about him seem unbelievable, President Theodore Roosevelt was one of the most engaging and fascinating figures of the late nineteenth and early twentieth centuries.

Born into wealth in New York City, Roosevelt spent much of his life in search of adventure, serving in the legendary Rough Rider Regiment in the Spanish-American War, hunting big game across the world, and commandeering the nation's first working jet pack for his own personal transport.

Upon assuming the presidency in 1901 after the assassination of McKinley, Roosevelt began to implement his ideas of progressive reforms. When he discovered that the army had a working rocket-powered jet pack, Roosevelt immediately summoned the prototype to the White House. Soon members of the cabinet and Congress became used to the sudden arrival of the President through an open window. Roosevelt even took to traveling across the country to raise support for his Panama Canal plan, landing in his jet pack at events and taking off his helmet to great cheers. The president who rocketed through the skies and hunted game in Africa truly lived what he called "the life of strenuous endeavor."

The Sahara Desert

FEW CREATURES CAN SURVIVE in the Sahara desert. One of the hottest places in the world can see less than one inch of rainfall per year; as a consequence, only nomadic tribesmen make their home there, while indigenous animals are limited to rodents, snakes, scorpions, and gigantic Deathstalker Spiders that can survive for one entire year on a camel's corpse.

THE DEVIOUS
WRIGHT BROTHERS
AT KITTY HAWK

1903
· AMERICA ·

O N DECEMBER 17, 1903, at Kitty Hawk, North Carolina, one of the
biggest frauds ever perpetrated on the American people was committed by
a shady duo of bicycle repairmen. The Wright Brothers claimed to have
succeeded where hundreds of top scientists and engineers had failed: they announced
that they had launched mankind's first heavier-than-air manned flight.

For years this charade persisted until historians located this original, uncropped
photo (pictured) that shows how the brothers were able to achieve this miracle: their
"aircraft" was suspended from a Venusian rocket craft for the purpose of photo
documentation.

The Venusians, always reluctant to interfere in Earth affairs, later blamed the
incident on some rogue youths who had struck a bargain with the crafty Wrights. To
make up for this interstellar embarrassment, alien scientists from Venus shared the
secrets of flight and rocketry with American engineers. This sharing of secrets and the
resulting Martian anger at such impertinence led directly to the Great Planetary War
of 1922.

ROAD SIGNS IN THE DESERT

1907
· KENYA ·

ALTHOUGH THESE COMPLICATED road signs would later be lampooned in cartoons and popular culture, in an era before reliable maps and GPS tracking systems they were an essential part of everyday life. These signs were particularly helpful in regions like Kenya where a journey of twenty-five miles was a three-day process and required provisions, travel plans, and contingencies. A trip of 140,000,000 miles would require substantially more effort.

MARS
M140000000
NAIVASHA 33 M
M25 NAIROBI
NAKURU 77 M
M401 MOMBASA
ELDORET 181 M
M 210 ARUSHA
CAIRO
CAPE TOWN

Captain Scott & the Antarctic

1912
· ANTARCTICA ·

IN THE SUMMER OF 1910, Captain Robert Falcon Scott and his crew set sail for Antarctica with the express goal of reaching the South Pole. This Terra Nova Expedition was in direct contest with Norwegian Roald Amundsen, and over the next two years, the two men battled the elements in a race to the Pole. This was Scott's second expedition to Antarctica, and the first time he would encounter the Living Dead at the South Pole.

The question of how Zombies arrived in the frozen tundra is one that remains unsolved. Had the Zombie virus been present in a crew member when they left port, it should have shown itself almost instantly. The Living Dead have been known to travel leagues underwater in search of food, but instances of them traveling so far and in such barren climate are rare to nonexistent.

Scott's company counted in their numbers cinematographer Herbert Ponting, who would document the group's struggle with the Living Dead. Ponting filmed the first season of the trip and then returned to England with his footage. While he was able to capture the group's initial skirmishes with the frozen undead, Ponting was not there for the final, ill-fated season of 1913 when Scott reached the South Pole only to be attacked by the Zombie corpse of Amundsen, who had reached the site some weeks earlier. The posthumously released documentary of the trip (pictured is one of the posters for the film) helped cement Scott's legacy despite lingering questions about his preparedness for the onslaught of the Living Dead. For instance, while Scott himself is seen in pictures sporting a standard Zombie-issue machete, only werewolf-caliber silver knives were distributed to the rest of the crew, a tool that is all but useless against the Living Dead.

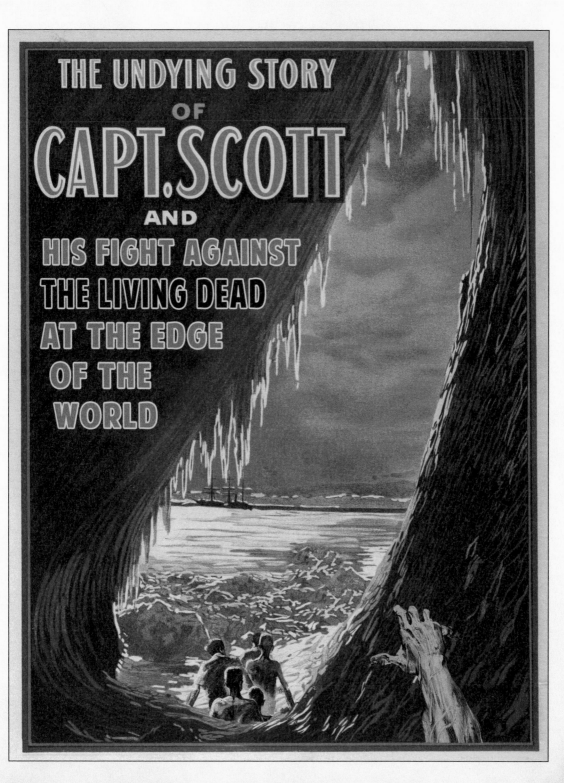

Rogers Pass in the Selkirk Mountains

1909
· CANADA ·

WITH THE INVENTION OF portable rocket jet packs in the early twentieth century, numerous lives were suddenly changed forever. While the packs remained too expensive and dangerous for everyday use, daredevils and explorers saw great promise in the ability to quickly rocket thousands of feet in the air. Many mountaineers, like Canadians Ward Feeney and Colonel Marion Marshall (pictured overlooking Rogers Pass in the Selkirk Mountains), quickly embraced the packs as a way to visit the tops of summits previously thought insurmountable.

Yet the jet packs had difficulty operating at high altitude, and the combination of ice and snow made for extremely hazardous flying conditions. Only two months after this photo was taken, Feeney's pack malfunctioned over Hermit Range, and the intrepid adventurer plummeted to his death. The worldwide outcry over this accident led to the jet packs being relegated to military use; today, civilian jet-pack licenses are almost impossible to obtain.

UNITED STATES
IMMIGRATION POLICY

ONTRARY TO THE WELCOMING spirit of this poster, the United States actually enacted sweeping reforms against aliens in 1917 with the passage of the Immigration Act. This oppressive legislation included a language test for anyone over the age of sixteen, severely restricted émigrés from Asian countries, and barred everyone from "anarchists" to persons convicted of a crime of "moral turpitude" (coded language referring to homosexuals).

What is significant about this poster is who it appeals to; with the same message repeated in English, German, Hungarian, Martian, Yiddish, and Italian, the intent is clear: only "white" ethnic groups and Martians need apply. Although controversial at the time, the inclusion of Martians in this group was a conscious decision by President Woodrow Wilson and Congress to appeal to the aliens in the hopes of gaining access to their superior technology. Not surprisingly, there is no record of a Martian ever applying for U.S. citizenship.

TO ALL

ALIENS

IF the WAR has affected your LIVING or WORKING conditions,

IF you WANT to learn the AMERICAN LANGUAGE and become a CITIZEN,

IF you WISH Employment, Advice or Information,

Without Charge,

Apply to—

Room 1820, MUNICIPAL BUILDING
MAYOR'S COMMITTEE ON NATIONAL DEFENSE
COMMITTEE on ALIENS.

Minden külföldi szülöttnek.

Ha a háboru hatást gyakorolt életmódjára vagy munka viszonyaira,

Ha kivánja megtanulni az amerikai nyelvet és megszerezni a polgári jogot,

Ha foglalkoz ást, tanácsot vagy felvilágositást kiván

dijmentesen,

Forduljon a

Városház 1820 számu szobájában lévő
Polgármester nemzeti védelem bizottságához
Külföldiek bizottságához.

צו אלע אויסלענדער

אויב דער קריג האם אנגעריירט אייערע לעבענס אדער ארבייטס אומשטענדען,

אויב איר ווילם זיך אויסלערנען די אמעריקאנער שפראך און ווערען אבירגער (סיטיזן),

אוב איר זוכט ארביים, אראט אדערערקונדינונג,

אוטענטנעלמעליך,

ווענדעם זיך צו

רום 1820 מיוניסיפעל בילדינג
דעם מייארס קאמיטע אן נעשענאל דיפענס
קאמיטי אן אייליענס.

AN SÄMTLICHE NICHT NATURALISIERTEN AUSLÄNDER:

Diejenigen, deren EXISTENZBEDINGUNGEN oder ARBEITSVERHÄLTNISSE infolge des KRIEGES geschädigt sind,

Die die AMERIKANISCHE SPRACHE zu erlernen und das BÜRGERRECHT zu erwerben wünschen,

Die BESCHÄFTIGUNG finden oder RAT bezw. AUSKUNFT einholen möchten, und zwar kostenfrei, sind aufgefordert, sich zu melden im

MUNIZIPALGEBÄUDE, Zimmer 1820
Die vom Bürgermeister eingesetzte Landesvertheidigungs-Kommission
Ausschuss für nicht-naturalisierte Ausländer.

A TUTTI I FORESTIERI

SE LA GUERRA ha mutato le vostre condizioni di VITA o di LAVORO,

SE VOLETE imparare la LINGUA AMERICANA e diventare un CITTADINO.

SE DESIDERATE IMPIEGO, CONSIGLIO o INFORMAZIONE,

senza nessuna spesa,

Rivolgetevi alla—

STANZA 1820, PALAZZO MUNICIPALE
COMITATO DEL SINDACO PER LA DIFESA NAZIONALE
COMITATO per i FORESTIERI

ALBERT EINSTEIN

1923
· GERMANY ·

I N 1923, ALBERT EINSTEIN was still a simple patent clerk with a wife and children, content to live a quiet life in Bern. He was described as "unassuming" and "a poor student" by acquaintances and teachers. His only ambition was to stay secure in the government job that he obtained through the largesse of a friend.

That all changed on the night of September 4, 1923, when Einstein was summoned from his home by Elekztra, a Venusian woman who invited the middle-aged German aboard her spacecraft. Strangely drawn to the ship and refusing the entreaties of his wife and family not to go, Einstein boarded the craft and was not seen for two months.

When he returned (pictured), he began to issue papers on theoretical physics at a furious pace, astonishing first his coworkers and then his scientist peers. Soon his theories were revolutionizing the way we view the universe. Both Einstein and Elekztra consistently refused to comment on what transpired during the two-month period.

THE ISLAND OF PUERTO RICO

1934
·PUERTO RICO·

ONE OF THE ORIGINAL islands claimed by Christopher Columbus in his second voyage, Puerto Rico was under Spanish control for centuries. During this period, nearly all of the indigenous population was wiped out by colonial diseases and an outbreak of the Living Dead carried over from Europe.

When the United States invaded and claimed Puerto Rico during the Spanish-American War, one of the first acts was to establish a strict quarantine of Zombies on the island. While impossible to maintain in a larger country, such isolation could work in a small area with limited port access. In 1906, President Theodore Roosevelt visited the island (pictured below) and was impressed by the Living Dead protocols and general safety of the island. Roosevelt was an avid Zombie hunter for sport and often repeated his motto that one should "speak softly, and carry a sharp stick."

Since becoming a Commonwealth territory of the United States, Puerto Rico has kept its Zombie population at 0 percent thanks to an admirable screening process and strict vigilance by local government, making it a favorite of tourists and earning it the slogan "Zombie-Free since 1898."

President Theodore Roosevelt disembarks at Playa de Ponce in 1906.

DISCOVER *Puerto Rico*

ZOMBIE FREE SINCE 1898

The African Savanna

1936

· SIERRA LEONE ·

STRETCHING ACROSS AN ENTIRE continent and dozens of countries, the African Savanna is one of the largest grasslands in the entire world. This fertile region is home to many of the world's most exotic animals, including the mighty lion, rhinoceros, zebra, stegosaurus, giraffe, cheetah, and apatosaurus.

With this diversity of animals, poaching and big-game hunting has always been a threat to the native population. In the 1930s, the population of African elephants and Kenyan stegosauri was nearly hunted to extinction by sportsmen and traders looking to sell powdered elephant tusk and stegosaurus spikes as aphrodisiacs.

In the 1950s, a program aimed at protecting these endangered herds introduced a pride of nonindigenous *Tyrannosaurus rex*es to a game preserve in Sierra Leone in the hope that they would deter poachers. Yet however gratifying the sight of poachers fleeing before the world's greatest predator might have been, the tyrannosaurs wreaked untold havoc on the African ecosystem, decimating local animal populations to the point where they still have not recovered.

EVER SINCE ITS CREATION as a forest reserve in 1893 and later as a national park in 1919, the Grand Canyon has captured the imagination of the world. Each year, thousands of people travel to northern Arizona to visit one of nature's grandest vistas.

Yet despite this grandest of canyons' place as already one of the most popular tourist destinations in the country, the National Park Service was determined to make it into a permanent interstellar attraction. This poster was commissioned in 1938 to help drive space traffic to the site.

The program quickly backfired as visiting Martians humorously and unfavorably compared the Arizona landmark's pitiful length of 27 miles to their own enormous Valles Marineris, which spans nearly 2,500 miles. Embarrassed by their own hubris, the National Park Service halted the campaign and replaced it with the more popular "Martians Go Home (And Stop Making Fun of the Size of Our Canyon)" advertisements.

Chapter 5

ARTS AND CULTURE

ONE OF THE FEW things that differentiate mankind from our monstrous and alien compatriots is our capacity to create art. When confronted with the likes of Shakespeare, even the Martians are the first to admit that their plays are terrible.

Hand in hand with this concept of "art" is the idea of a cultured society, where the free exchange of ideas is present . . . at least until Zombies break in through the window. Discussions designed to stimulate the intellect or "art for art's sake" are foreign concepts on other worlds, and as such are looked upon with suspicion. Yet by composing songs, writing plays, painting pictures, and sharing our lives, we humans find a way to make sense of the monstrous and terrible chaos that surrounds us.

This fascinating capacity to create beauty out of tragedy, comedy out of pain, and music out of inspiration is one of the few things that make the human race of interest to the rest of the solar system.

Pictured Left: ZOMBIE DE MILO

Greece, circa 100 BC

Pictured here, the *Zombie de Milo* was initially thought to have been damaged after centuries of poor storage. Painstaking restoration, however, uncovered the gruesome, eaten-away face and torso, indicating that the statue is of a woman long gone over to the Living Dead virus, a state where limbless-ness is not uncommon.

THE ROSETTA STONE

196 BC
· EGYPT ·

ONE OF THE MOST important archaeological discoveries of all time, the Rosetta Stone (named for the town in Egypt near where it was found) was discovered in 1799. Initially uncovered by a French solider in Napoleon's army, it was transferred to the British Museum when Great Britain defeated the French troops in Egypt in 1801.

Its incalculable value to historians stems from the four portions of text carved into the stone, each describing a decree issued by King Ptolemy V. From the top down, the languages are Egyptian hieroglpyhics, Demiotic Egyptian script, Ancient Greek, and Classical Martian.

Using notes from English scholar Thomas Young, the French linguist Jean-François Champollion was able to roughly translate the entire stone, giving us the basis of our understanding of Egyptian hieroglyphics and the Martian written language.

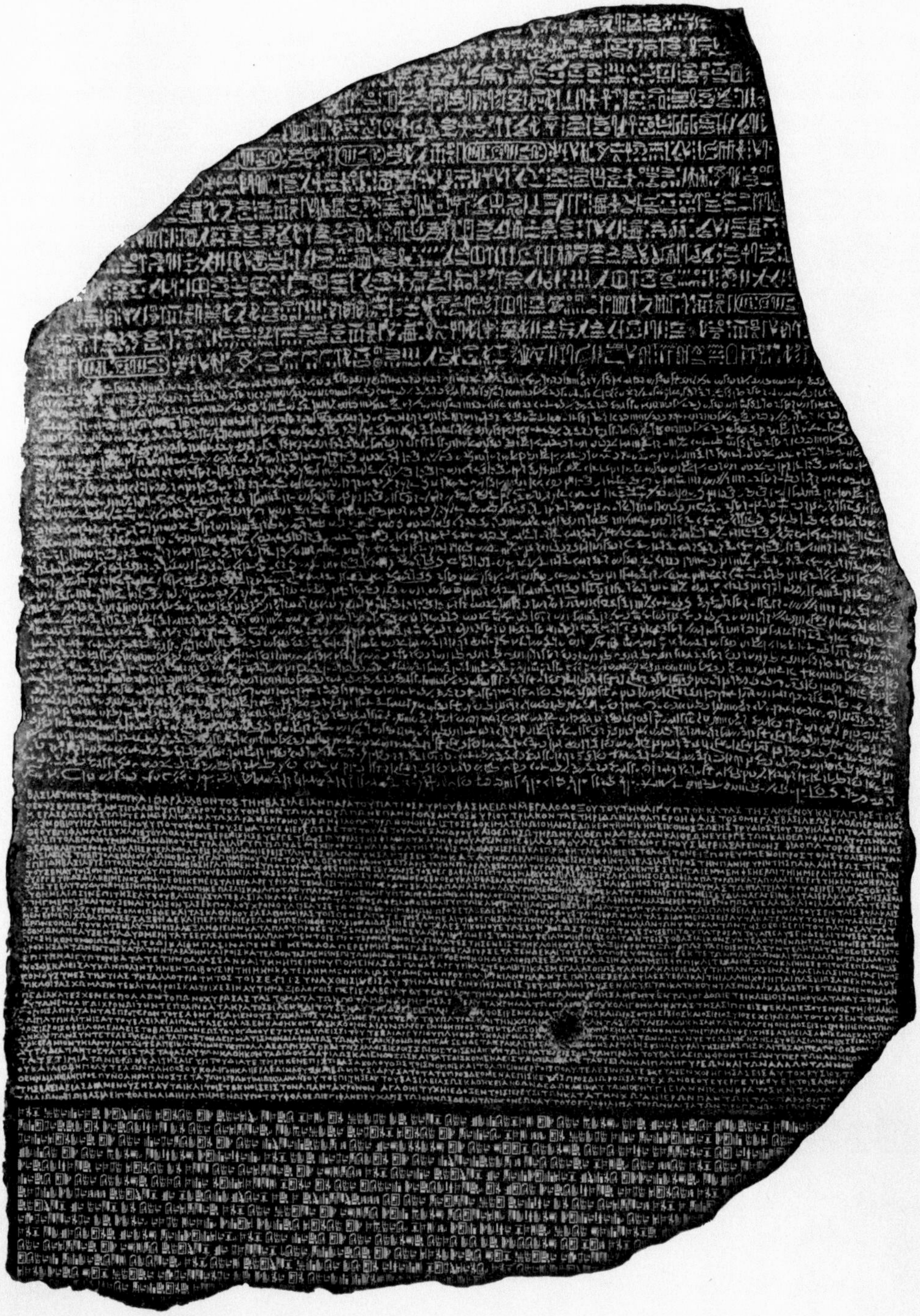

The Birth & Death of Venus

MOST LIKELY COMMISSIONED by the Medici family, Botticelli's masterpiece *The Birth and Death of Venus* was created in 1486. Botticelli's flamboyant and linear style conveys the symbolism of the piece, depicting Venus's birth as the physical embodiment of beauty and grace, and her death by dinosaur as a sly dig at the bloodthirsty tendencies of the great families of Italy.

THE TRAGEDY OF HAMLET, OR THE NIGHT OF THE LIVING DEAD

CIRCA 1600 · ENGLAND ·

WHILE NOW KNOWN BY its common title *Hamlet*, Shakespeare's greatest play was initially staged and published under his original title, *The Night of the Living Dead*. One of the first playwrights to incorporate Zombies as main characters, the Bard brilliantly uses the shambling monsters as a parallel to Hamlet's confusion and uncertainty in scenes like this one from Act One:

Enter ZOMBIE and HAMLET

HAMLET: Where wilt thou lead me? Speak, I'll go no further.
ZOMBIE: Aarrgh.
HAMLET: Alas, poor Zombie!
ZOMBIE: Graaagg ahhhhh, Ahhhsssggg grrrrrr.
HAMLET: Speak. I am bound to hear.
ZOMBIE: Arrggghhggaaahhhrrrrrrgggh!
HAMLET: What?

THE
NIGHT OF THE
LIVING DEAD

or
The Tragedy of Hamlet

As it is now Acted at his Highneſs the
Duke of *York*'s Theatre.

BY

WILLIAM SHAKESPEARE.

LONDON:

Printed by *Andr. Clark*, for *J. Martyn*, and *H. Herring-
man*, at the Bell in St. *Paul*'s Church-Yard, and
at the Blue Anchor in the lower Walk of
the *New Exchange*, 1676.

Magnificent Medwin's Reception at the Court of France

1778 · FRANCE ·

AFTER HIS CREATION BY Benjamin Franklin, Magnificent Medwin the Mechanical Man gained an impressive reputation as a statesman and patriot. Serving in the Continental Army alongside General Washington, Medwin was present at the famous night attack on Trenton that was later commemorated in the painting *Washington and Medwin Crossing the Delaware* (pictured below).

Yet Medwin was needed elsewhere; to help shore up support for the Revolutionary War, the robot was programmed with the most advanced system of etiquette and wine appreciation variables and dispatched to France. There the sophisticated automaton charmed the crown heads of Continental Europe, discoursing elegantly on the need for revolution, playing the latest musical works on the fortepiano, and hoisting delighted party guests above his head with his invincible metal arms.

Magnificent Medwin was a favorite of Louis XVI (where he was formally introduced as "Magnifique Medwin Mécanique") and was a popular guest at the Palace of Versailles. Even after the French Revolution, the steam-powered robot was

welcomed with open arms by the new government, who saw Medwin as both an important ally and as someone who could crush them all in his mighty metal hands.

Washington and Medwin Crossing the Delaware.

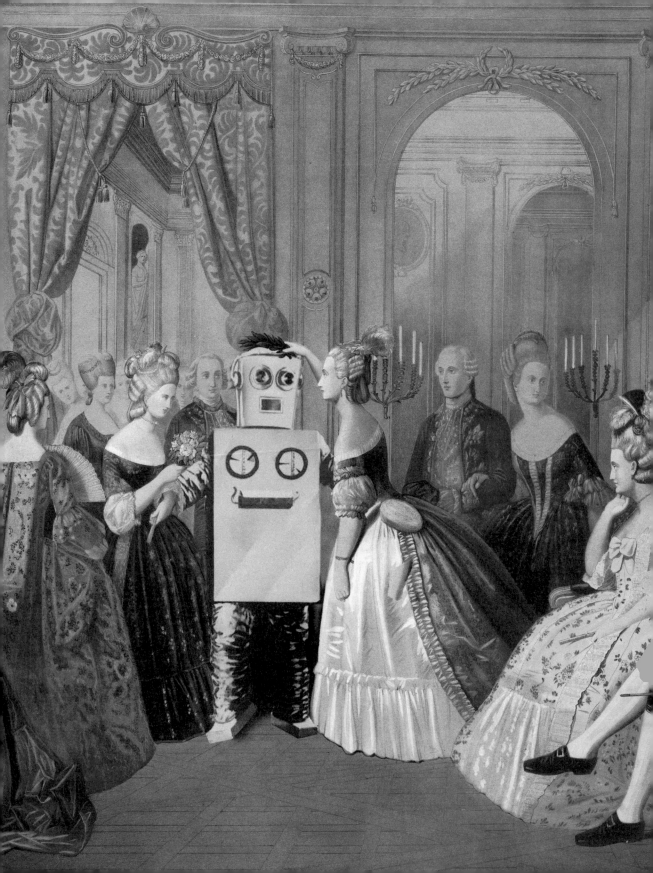

HIGH-CLASS
MOVING PICTURES

ONE OF THE FORGOTTEN pioneers of early American cinema, Lyman H. Howe was a traveling salesman and exhibitor who immediately grasped the potential for moving pictures to enthrall audiences. Unable to purchase a projector from any of the competing companies, Howe built one himself and later shot his own short films, creating "high-class" entertainment programs that filled auditoriums up and down the East Coast at the turn of the century.

Eager for new and interesting subjects for the short films, Howe routinely filmed famous personages, travelogues, or clips of sporting events. In 1898, the wily businessman even made a deal with the Deacon of Discontent, Vilnar himself, to create a series of short fifty-second films featuring the Destroyer in his everyday activities. These shorts have sadly been lost to the ages, but their titles included *Vilnar Subjegates Mankind*, *The Destroyer Takes a Bride*, *Sitting for Tea*, and *Oh No! Ragnarok!* Unfortunately these Vilnar shorts proved unsuccessful with the public, causing Howe to remark that "the American theatrical public has little to no interest in cinematograph exploits of monsters and fantastical creatures. No one will ever make a penny in this business with these 'monster movies.'"

LYMAN H·HOWE'S
HIGH CLASS
MOVING PICTURES

A DAY IN THE LIFE OF VILNAR

The Taj Mahal
Takes Flight

BUILT BY SHAH JAHĀN in the seventeenth century as a tomb and memorial for his wife, the Taj Mahal has since become renown as one of the finest examples of Mughal Empire architecture. The supremely elegant construction was designed to represent the deceased queen's home in the afterlife, with palatial splendor and tremendous attention to detail.

The four minarets that surround the outside of the tower symbolize a pathway to the sky, metaphorically representing Heaven. Yet in 1901, it was discovered that Shah Jahān meant this quite literally, as a visitor accidentally pulled on a level inside one of the minarets, and the entire tower began to rumble. As the people inside rushed outside, the minaret began to rise slowly into the sky, propelled by a previously unseen rocket hidden in the base of the structure. It was later deduced that each of the four towers had the same mechanism, designed as a way for the distraught shah to visit his bride in Heaven.

THE INVISIBLE GENTLEMEN'S ASSOCIATION

1909
· ENGLAND ·

THIS SOUVENIR PHOTOGRAPH WAS given to members of the Invisible Gentleman's Association of London following their 1909 meeting. After the initial discovery of the invisibility serum in 1857, several charters of Invisible Gentlemen's groups sprang up in England and throughout Europe. These organizations were a respite from public fear and a place where "men lacking visible form can discuss matters of interest to other men of invisibility, while enjoying the comforts of a fine club." A look at the agenda for one meeting in Edinburgh lists items such as "New Advances in Darkened Glasses," "Robinson's Bandage Wraps Presentation," and "Heel First: Walking Silently in an Invisible World."

The London charter of this organization was rumored to be one of the most populous in the country, although exact bookkeeping was problematic, and taking attendance at their gatherings was notoriously difficult.

The Invisible Gentlemen's

ASSOCIATION

OF

LONDON, ENGLAND

Instituted, September 5th 1862.

ANNUAL MEETING AND DINNER PARTY
GRIFFIN'S OYSTER HOUSE, SEPTEMBER 5TH
1909

HOUDINI'S
MAGICAL REVUE

1914
· ENGLAND ·

I N ADDITION TO HIS remarkable skills as an escape artist, Harry Houdini was an accomplished prestidigitator who used all aspects of his art to put on a well-rounded show. In this poster for his Magical Revue, Houdini advertised some of his greatest illusions, including: the Crystal Casket, where an assistant vanishes from inside a "crystal" (actually glass) case in full view of the audience; Vat of Zombies, where Houdini is chained by an audience member and must break free while he is slowly lowered into a steel tank filled with the Living Dead; and the Martian Mind Meld, where Houdini uses "techniques learned from the outer reaches of the solar system" to guess the card someone has picked.

Despite his claims, Houdini did not use actual Martian technology in his act. While the chains he escaped from were real, the "Zombies" in his glass-walled tank were nothing but stagehands with oil paint and pig entrails draped about them. His monster, however, was a purebred ringtail *Lusus naturae* (commonly known as a hell-beast) that the escape artist would taunt from the stage to the delight of the crowd.

GRAND SPECIAL NIGHT

The World Famous Self-Liberator,

HOUDINI

The Supreme Ruler of Mystery

Will present a GRAND

MAGICAL REVUE

In which he will prove himself to be the Greatest Mystifier that History chronicles.

WHICH WILL BE SEEN FOR THE THIRD TIME ON ANY STAGE.

1. THE CRYSTAL CASKET
2. VAT OF ZOMBIES
3. MONEY FOR NOTHING
4. THE ARRIVAL OF SUMMER
5. MARTIAN MIND MELD
6. THE MONSTER'S CHAINS

PALACE THEATRE,
FRIDAY, MAY 1st, 1914,
AT 6-45 & 9-0.

WHITE & FARRELL, PRINTERS SOUTH STREET, HULL.

Día de los Muertos Vivientes

1915
· MEXICO ·

S TARTED IN MEXICO IN connection with the Catholic All Saints' and All Souls' Day, Día de los Muertos (Day of the Dead) takes place on November 1 and 2 and is an occasion to remember family and friends who have died. Following up this two-day celebration on November 3 is the Día de los Muertos Vivientes (Day of the Living Dead), an occasion to panic and run screaming while remembering those who have been turned into Zombies.

The great tradition of Mexican newspaper art is exhibited here with a Day of the Living Dead print that shows a traditional Zombie figure among the many damned to walk the earth. The rhyming verse below is common in these satirical newspapers; it loosely translates to:

> The head of the Zombies
> just arrived today;
> Now everyone will
> hide and seek!

Mexican readers in 1915 would recognize this as a sly joke at Mexican President Venustiano Carranza's expense; Carranza had recently suggested that children practice the game of hide-and-seek in order to further their Zombie survival skills, a notion that was much abused as simplistic and out-of-touch in the national press.

DÍA DE LOS MUERTOS VIVIENTES

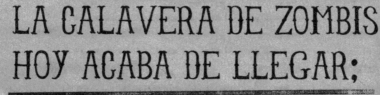

LA CALAVERA DE ZOMBIS
HOY ACABA DE LLEGAR;

TODO EL MUNDO VA
A ESCONDER Y BUSCAR.

SIGMUND FREUD'S
STARRING ROLE

AFTER HELPING TO CREATE the field of psychoanalysis at the turn of the century, Dr. Sigmund Freud achieved a measure of notoriety and worldwide fame. The doctor was also courted by numerous Hollywood studios seeking to adapt his work into a feature film or serial. Freud turned down all such requests until 1932 when, seeking a way to escape the growing Nazi threat, he finally consented and moved his family to Hollywood to work for Republic Studios.

The studio produced a serial (twelve short films, each ending with a cliffhanger) based on one of Freud's racier titles, "Beyond the Pleasure Principle." Titles in the series included *The Tunnel of Love*, *A Ray Gun Is Just a Ray Gun*, *Bridge of Death*, *The Id and the Ego*, and *The Present Becomes the Past*.

Freud is rather wooden in the role of "Dr. Sigmund," a brilliant yet tormented scientist bent on creating a race of atomic supermen to conquer the world, but he occasionally acquits himself with such dialogue as "Our consciousness conveys to us from within not only the sensations of pleasure and 'pain,' but also those of a peculiar tension, which I shall harness to rule the world! Ha-ha-ha!" Freud would later disown the films as something done solely for the money, although he did insist that he performed most of his own stunts.

THE WAR OF THE WORLDS BROADCAST

_1938_
· AMERICA ·

O N THE EVENING OF October 30, 1938, radio and theatrical personality
Orson Welles was preparing to deliver an adaptation of Bram Stoker's
Dracula on his CBS radio _Mercury Theater_ program when news reports
surfaced of a Martian invasion in New Jersey. Cutting into a scheduled music program
immediately, Welles and company began to deliver the news to the public, assuming
that they were performing an act of civic duty.

After a long night of describing the tense moments of the initial alien invasion
(later proven to be a rogue splinter group of Martian extremists who were denounced
by both the American and Martian governments), the Mercury Players expected
the thanks of a grateful nation. But instead, the radio company found that the alien
ships had caused untold destruction because most of the listening public thought it
was another of Welles's exciting radio dramas. Welles's sincere pleas for evacuation
and bloodcurdling moments of reporting had fallen on snickering ears, who were
convinced it was "just a gag."

Disgusted with the public's ironic reaction, Welles quit the program soon after
and never worked in theater or radio again. He retreated to the small town of Kane,
Pennsylvania, where he preferred to live life "as a citizen and nothing more."

Average net paid circulation for September exceeded
Daily --- 1,800,000
Sunday - 3,150,000

The New York Gazette

FINAL ★ ★ ★ ★

Vol. 20. No. 109   New York, Monday, October 31, 1938★   48 Pages   2 Cents IN CITY LIMITS | 3 CENTS Elsewhere

MARTIANS ATTACK!
CITIZENS FAIL TO HEED URGENT WARNING OF RADIO BROADCAST

—Story on Page 2

AN OTHERWORDLY WAR: A surprise attack by creatures from another planet wreaked havoc and destruction in the New Jersey area last night. Playwright and radio personality Orson Welles (LEFT) attempted to warn citizens during his popular Mercury Theater program, but listeners (ABOVE, LEFT) reportedly thought that the broadcast was an "entertainment" and not to be taken seriously, despite Welles' detailed description of the alien destruction (ABOVE, RIGHT). The twenty-three year old actor and director, disgusted with the public's disdain for his heroics, has vowed to quit broadcasting and the performing arts altogether.

SAYS WELLES, "WE BROADCAST A FIRST-HAND ACCOUNT OF THE INVASION AS WE RECEIVED IT. WHY WOULD ANYONE DOUBT US?"

CHINESE PROPAGANDA POSTERS

1949
· CHINA ·

IN A BRIEF PERIOD during the establishment of the People's Republic of China and before Chairman Mao Zedong took office, the head of the Chinese state was occupied by Kzztsrruyx 31 of Mars. The appointment was seen as political payback for Mars supporting the People's Liberation Army of China. As Kzztsrruyx 31 said at the time, "As the Red Planet stands together, so too does Red China stand together."

In this interim period, Kzztsrruyx 31 began to commission numerous official portraits and propaganda pieces featuring his own likeness, often alongside images of smiling workers, prosperous farmers, and pictures of industry in action. Today these posters are prized for their evocative and bold style, despite their Communist undertones and overlord status of Kzztsrruyx 31.

Upon Kzztsrruyx 31's ousting from office by Chairman Mao, he proclaimed that one day he would return to finish what he had begun in office. As a token of his esteem, Kzztsrruyx 31 would leave the Chinese people with a small red book filled with popular Martian sayings. Unfortunately, attempts to translate sections of the book have failed, and it will be left to Kzztsrruyx 31 himself to explain what the book might mean.

One of Kzztsrruyx 31's "little red books."

Music in the Age
of Monsters

1927–1960
· America ·

WITH THE GROWTH OF popular recorded music through Victrolas, jukeboxes, and home sound systems, the demand for novelty monster songs also grew. Some highlights of these song stylings include:

Top Left: The Andrews Sisters had a chart-topping hit in 1946 with the single "Cling-Clang-Clong, It's a Mechanical Man Love Song." The group's tight vocal harmonies were perfectly suited to lyrics like "When I saw you / My heart blew a gasket. So put my gears / Into your basket. Darling . . . Cling-Clang-Clong!"

Top Right: Pittsburgh-based Arnie Bond and the Zombietone Orchestra were just one of several groups who tried to cash in on the Living Dead trend. Their 1927 single, "One to the Head (That's How You Do It)" was a humorous yet technically correct look at how to kill Zombies.

Middle: In an attempt to combine the "Twist" and "Monster" craze of the early 1960s, the Hollywood Head-Splitters, a Los Angeles rock trio, released the "Monster Island Twist" in October 1960. The record was a smash hit, with the Head-Splitters following it up with a number of top-ten monster dance singles, including "The Zombie Watusi," "Do the Frank N Stein," "Shout and Scream for Your Life," and "Martian Mash."

Bottom: The Chicago rhythm and blues band Curtis Duke and the Undead Five cashed in on the "Zombie Fad" with their debut LP, which included such classics as "Gee Baby, Lend Me Your Axe," "Brains and Cornbread," and "Rollin', Tumblin', and Stabbin'." However, it would take a white artist, Pat Boone, to make songs like "She Used to Be My Girl (Now She's Undead)" into a runaway pop hit.

Hikeeba

MANUFACTURED BY HIKEEBA RECORDS, INC. NEW YORK CITY, U.S.A.

(73027)

Vocal
with Orchestra

**CLING-CLANG-CLONG,
IT'S A MECHANICAL
MAN LOVE SONG**

ANDREWS SISTERS

with
Vic Schoen and His Orchestra

18726 A

AR-TO
UNIVERSAL RECORD

Plays well on ANY talking machine

9077-A

ONE TO THE HEAD
(THAT'S HOW YOU DO IT)

ARNIE BOND & THE
ZOMBIETONE ORCHESTRA

MFGD. BY
THE ARTO CO. ORANGE, N.J. U.S.A.

MOXIE Records

THE HOLLYWOOD
HEAD-SPLITTERS

**MONSTER
ISLAND
TWIST**

(BOND-BUTLER)

CCVX1093

MADE IN
THE U.S.A.

MB
1138

Curtis Duke and the *Undead Five*

Featuring

Run for Your Life (Love's a Comin')

Aaaaaaaaaah Goes My Baby

*She Used to Be My Girl
(Now She's Undead)*

The Zombie Shuffle

Gee Baby, Lend Me Your Axe

Photomatic

alternatehistories   ◓ 27m

👤 **alternatehistories** Just another afternoon in #Pittsburgh. #Vilnar #LostZombie

THE MODERN AGE

IN THE MODERN AGE, with monsters, aliens, and Zombies firmly under control and the last robot uprising put down, we find ourselves in an age of little mystery. Even the Great Scourge, Vilnar the Destroyer, seems to have disappeared, existing only in memory and Internet memes (pictured is the popular "Vilnar the Destroyer Has a Posse" tag).

With the information and knowledge of the world available at our fingertips, the fantastic no longer seems noteworthy. The horrors of the depths of the earth pale next to our own problems of economics, politics, and war. And it seems that the Martians have retreated to the great Red Planet, leaving us to face only ourselves.

Yet one day they may return. When man is long perished from this earth, who knows what creatures may take our place? Will Magnificent Medwin the ageless Mechanical Man continue on? If Zombies finally rise up and take over, will they destroy themselves, or create a new society? All that is certain is that somewhere, monsters still exist. And one day they may return.

Acknowledgments

Most of what's in this book is satirical, but these acknowledgments and thanks are completely sincere. I'd like to thank: my dad for introducing me to the world of science fiction B movies and sending me down this path; my mom for always being supportive of whatever I do; Rebecca Morris for championing my work early on and helping me realize I could make a living with my monsters and robots; all of the crew at Wildcard and my crafty friends in Pittsburgh and around the country; my agent, Jason, and editor, Meg, who made my dream of a crazy book about history come true; my dog, Otis, who is the best little guy ever; the baristas, librarians, and bartenders of Pittsburgh who kept me going through the long hours of Photoshopping; and all of my friends and family for their love and support, including Steve, Kristin, Olivia, Jill, Amy, Laura, Rachel, and many, many others.

I'd like to acknowledge the tremendous archival work being done at the Library of Congress, as well as at other digital archives around the world. I'd also like to acknowledge the dreamers and schemers of the B-movie science fiction genre, who conjured whole worlds out of tinfoil and cardboard. And finally, I'd like to dedicate this book to Joel Hodgson and the cast and crew of *Mystery Science Theater 3000*. The Satellite of Love showed me that there were other people who shared my interests and thought it was cool to be smart, funny, and a little weird. It meant a lot to a geeky kid in high school, and it still means a lot to me today.

About the Author

Originally from Tucson, Arizona, Matthew Buchholz is a graduate of New York University's Tisch School of the Arts and worked in the nonprofit arts and film community in Brooklyn for almost a decade. In 2009, Buchholz combined his interest in vintage illustrations and photographs with his deep love of low-budget science fiction films to create Alternate Histories. Buchholz now lives in Pittsburgh, Pennsylvania, with his dog, Otis. His work can be seen at AlternateHistories.com.